D0928986

PARKS

Our Shared Heritage

The Phoenix Park, Dublin & The Royal Parks, London

OPW
Oifig na nOibreacha Poiblí
The Office of Public Works

THE HEARSUM
COLLECTION

THE
ROYAL
PARKS

Published in 2017 by the Government
Publications Office
The Office of Public Works
Jonathan Swift Street
Trim
County Meath
Ireland

to coincide with the exhibition

*Parks: Our Shared Heritage.
The Phoenix Park, Dublin and
The Royal Parks, London*

7 April 2017 – 28 May 2017
in Farmleigh, Dublin, and

27 July 2017 – 11 August 2017
in Mall Galleries, London

Project Co-ordinator
Margaret Gormley

Exhibition Curators
Dr John A McCullen
Rheme Fordham

Exhibition Designers
Steven McNamara
Jurga Rakauskaite

Catalogue Project Team
Margaret Gormley
Bridgeen Kelly
Raychel Coyle
Niamh Guihen
Pat Blair
Dr John A McCullen
Rheme Fordham
Daniel Hearsum

Catalogue Co-ordinators
Margaret Gormley
Marie Harpur

Catalogue Text Editor
Elizabeth Mayes

Catalogue Designer
Paul Martin

Printed and bound in Ireland
Printrun

ISBN: 978-1-4064-2947-3

Le ceannach díreach ó
FOILSEACHÁIN RIALTAIS,
52 FAICHE STIABHNA, BAILE ÁTHA
CLIATH 2
(Teil: 01 – 0761106834 nó 1890 213434;
Fax 0761106843)
nó trí aon díoltóir leabhar.

To be purchased from
GOVERNMENT PUBLICATIONS,
52 ST. STEPHEN'S GREEN, DUBLIN 2.
(Tel: 0761106834 or 1890 213434;
Fax: 0761106843)
or through any bookseller.

EXHIBITION VENUES

Parks: Our Shared Heritage.
The Phoenix Park, Dublin
and The Royal Parks, London

Farmleigh Gallery,
Phoenix Park, Dublin 15, Ireland
7 April 2017 – 28 May 2017

Mall Galleries/Federation of British Artists Ltd,
Mall Galleries, The Mall, London SW1
27 July 2017 – 11 August 2017

FARMLEIGH GALLERY

MALL GALLERIES

'We love parks to play our sports in.'
Aimee, age 13 and Eoin, age 15

TABLE OF CONTENTS

'THIS EXHIBITION INTRODUCES THE PUBLIC TO THE MAGIC OF THESE MEMORABLE PARKS.'

PREFACE

This exhibition, *Parks: Our Shared Heritage. The Phoenix Park, Dublin and The Royal Parks, London*, is a unique collaboration between the Office of Public Works and the Royal Parks and chronicles, for the first time ever, the rich artistic and social history of these magnificent Parks, for over three centuries.

The Phoenix Park was established as a royal deer park in 1662 by one of Ireland's most illustrious Viceroys, James Butler, Duke of Ormonde, on behalf of King Charles II. Today this historic landscape, one of international importance, has over 10 million visitors annually. The Office of Public Works is also responsible for managing State-owned National Monuments and Historic Properties, including two UNESCO World Heritage sites: Brú na Bóinne (Newgrange) in County Meath and Skellig Michael, County Kerry.

The world-renowned Royal Parks engage the public in so many ways, whether it be with their beautiful horticultural displays in St James's Park or in observing nature and biodiversity in Richmond Park.

The magnificent surroundings of Farmleigh Gallery provide an ideal backdrop for this exhibition in Dublin. Likewise, the Mall Galleries in the heart of London is a pivotal venue to showcase these masterpieces that have been so carefully curated.

To everyone who inspired, encouraged and helped us to assemble this wonderful exhibition, I would like to say a huge thank you, especially to the Hearsum Collection, which provided so many of the splendid paintings, images and artefacts of the eight Royal Parks, and to those other institutions and individuals who contributed to the exhibition in so many ways.

Our shared heritage with the United Kingdom has many strands. Our friends and colleagues in the Royal Parks and at the Hearsum Collection have been passionate and enthusiastic from the outset. Without such input the delivery of such a dynamic cultural exhibition on both sides of the Irish Sea would simply not have been possible. We look forward to future collaborations.

This exhibition introduces the public to the magic of these memorable parks. I sincerely hope that you enjoy it and that you will be inspired to explore for yourself these wondrous historic Parks, now, and into the future.

Maurice Buckley
Chairman
The Office of Public Works

'THE PARKS FEATURED HERE ARE AMONG
THE VERY BEST IN THE WORLD.'

FOREWORD

I am delighted to support this exhibition which celebrates the glories of the Royal Parks and Phoenix Park.

The Parks featured here are among the very best in the world. Over the years, artists have sought to capture the essence of what makes these places so special and beloved. In this exhibition some remarkable pieces of art and craft have been assembled to give a picture of both the variety of landscape and architecture in these wonderful parks, as well as the bonds and shared heritage between the United Kingdom and the Republic of Ireland.

The Royal Parks estate includes eight parks covering five thousand acres, each with its own distinctive personality and history. They are known across the world, whether, like St James's and Green Park, through coverage of ceremonial events, or like Hyde Park, with its long tradition as a place of public protest at Speakers' Corner or, more recently, as the host of global events such as the Live 8 concert. Greenwich Park is home to the Meridian Line which separates the eastern and western hemispheres, while Regent's Park is home not only to one of the country's best rose gardens but also to the capital's only open-air theatre. Nestled on the Thames, Richmond and Bushy Parks are equally special and much loved by visitors for their natural landscapes, biodiversity and deer herds.

The Parks were originally used as royal hunting grounds, but in earlier times they offered sanctuary to those fleeing the Black Death. More recently they have provided space for housing and hospitals during wartime. Today they are public amenity spaces, open for everyone to enjoy, catering for a wide range of activities.

In addition to their rich history, the Parks, above all, offer us an inherited privilege of natural beauty, whether it be a quiet meadow to share with family, a lakeside path on which to stroll and relax or grassland and woodland in which to seek that elusive moment of inspiration.

Around 77 million people now visit the Royal Parks every year. London would simply not be London without them. Likewise, Phoenix Park is one of the jewels of Dublin and a place I love.

With a collection procured from across the globe, this exhibition offers a fascinating insight into the rich heritage of the Royal Parks and Phoenix Park, shedding light on secret histories and personal connections to some of their well-known visitors and patrons.

I would like to offer particular thanks to the Hearsum Collection for its contribution to curating this exhibition and, crucially, for providing many of the items on show. I am also grateful to colleagues in the Office of Public Works for their huge support and generosity.

It has been a pleasure to work with our friends in the Republic of Ireland on this project. I hope it will encourage those on both sides of the Irish Sea to seek out these remarkable places. Our shared interests in environmental conservation, art and historical monuments, and in preserving a legacy for future generations, have cemented a like-minded relationship. I hope this is also the beginning of even closer and more fruitful links between the Royal Parks and Phoenix Park.

Andrew Scattergood
Chief Executive
The Royal Parks

‘WE ARE DEEPLY GRATEFUL TO THE OFFICE OF PUBLIC WORKS IN DUBLIN AND THE ROYAL PARKS IN LONDON FOR THEIR WHOLEHEARTED SUPPORT.’

THE HEARSUM COLLECTION

Some research in 1996 to inform a restoration project revealed that the heritage material of these much loved Royal Parks was scattered and inaccessible. This seemed wrong and so its repatriation became a hobby which grew into a passion and then a charity.

In 2007 we partnered with the Royal Parks and Friends of Richmond Park to open a trial visitor centre to find out what interested park visitors. It has been so popular that a much larger centre is planned. Credit for this success goes to the 70 volunteers who operate it with tremendous enthusiasm and dedication.

While I have had the joy of trawling the globe for interesting acquisitions, these would have fallen into useless disarray without the hard work of our history project volunteers and our professional curators, Rheme Fordham and Sue Barber.

These teams have achieved so much. Some 8,500 items have been catalogued and digitised, enabling an array of activities to share the rich heritage. Exhibitions are on display in Richmond Park and local schools. Over 100 talks and guided walks have been delivered by our trustees and partners.

A video featuring Sir David Attenborough was well received and a longer version is in production. The exhibition *Deer in the City*, supported by the Heritage Lottery Fund, explained the surreal oddity of wild deer herds in a capital city. It attracted 14,000 visitors in four weeks, with excellent feedback and requests for more in the same vein.

Many partnerships have developed, none warmer than our friendship with our colleagues from Phoenix Park, the sister park to Richmond Park. Over a thoroughly enjoyable dinner, Margaret Gormley asked, 'Daniel, would you bring this lovely collection over to Dublin?' and so the exhibition was born and simultaneously baptised.

It is a privilege to display some examples at Farmleigh and the Mall Galleries. We are deeply grateful to the Office of Public Works in Dublin and the Royal Parks in London for their wholehearted support.

We very much hope that you enjoy the exhibition as much as we have enjoyed its creation and we would really value your feedback.

Daniel Hearsum
Chairman
The Hearsum Collection
daniel@pl.org.uk

'THE PHOENIX PARK IS UNIQUE IN IRELAND AND CAN BE COMPARED TO REGENT'S PARK IN LONDON, THE BOIS DE BOULOGNE IN PARIS AND CENTRAL PARK IN NEW YORK.'

THE PHOENIX PARK

Even though the formation of Ireland's only royal deer park commenced in 1662, today Phoenix Park extends to over 700 hectares and represents a unique natural and cultural landscape that is both a historic park and an urban park. It provides a setting for a range of activities and amenities and acts as a location for a number of important public institutions and residences. As a natural and built park, enclosed over 300 years ago by a demesne wall, Phoenix Park is unique in Ireland. Its location, size and use can be compared to similar large parks in other cities, including Regent's Park in London, the Bois de Boulogne in Paris and Central Park in New York.

Research has shown that Neolithic and Early Bronze Age Man had long associations with the lands that now form Phoenix Park. Fifty percent of all mammal species found in Ireland occur within the Park and over 40 percent of all bird species occurring in Ireland have been recorded therein. A herd of wild fallow deer have roamed the Park since the 1660s. There are 25 different habitats and 6 different types of woodland. Almost all the semi-natural grassland in Dublin is found in Phoenix Park.

The Park has over 25 kilometres of roads, 17 kilometres of cycle trails, 27 kilometres of footpaths and 11 kilometres of perimeter wall. It caters for an average of 9 million car journeys per year, the majority of which are merely passing through. It is essential that the sensitive finite resource of Phoenix Park is sustainably managed and guided by the Phoenix Park Conservation Management Plan.

The cultural heritage of Phoenix Park enriches people's lives, often providing a deep and inspirational sense of connection to history and landscape. It provides a sense of place, locations for community cohesion and social inclusion, promotes cross-cultural enjoyment and space for over 2,300 recreational events. The Park is also good medicine, in that it provides numerous opportunities for green exercise which helps us all to lead healthier lifestyles. The major role of the Park in the tourism economy at local, national and international levels is often undervalued. The range of science and learning experiences are numerous.

The long-term vision for Phoenix Park combines its protection, conservation, enjoyment and tranquillity as an important unique historic landscape for the residents of Dublin and visitors to Ireland. Given the international significance of the Park, it will continue to be a place, managed by the Office of Public Works, where people go to experience heritage, culture and nature, comparable to the best parks in the world

It is hoped that this exhibition will foster a better understanding and appreciation of historic parks, where successive generations have toiled and places where current and future generations will be uplifted and inspired to reap the benefits of these wonderful parks.

Margaret Gormley
Chief Park Superintendent
The Office of Public Works

'I WOULD LIKE TO ACKNOWLEDGE ALL THESE INSTITUTIONS, FOUNDATIONS, ORGANISATIONS, PRIVATE COLLECTIONS AND INDIVIDUALS WHO ASSISTED WITH THIS MAGNIFICENT EXHIBITION.'

ACKNOWLEDGEMENTS

I would like to express my deep gratitude to the team at the Hearsum Collection in Richmond Park for their skill, dedication and foresight in collecting historical material on the Royal Parks and for sharing it with us, as part of the exhibition *Parks: Our Shared Heritage. The Phoenix Park, Dublin and The Royal Parks, London* – Daniel Hearsum, Chairman and Rheme Fordham, Curator. My thanks also to the Hearsum Collection trustees, staff and volunteers.

We are indebted to Andrew Scattergood, Chief Executive, and Loyd Grossman, Chairman of the Royal Parks, for their collaboration and support of this project from the onset. My thanks to David McLaren, Mark Wasilewski and all the Royal Parks staff, contractors and volunteers who look after these wonderful places. I would like to acknowledge the supporting role of Mike Fitt and the Royal Parks Guild.

To the team at the Mall Galleries, my thanks for all your help in planning and hosting the London element of the exhibition.

I am particularly grateful to Dr John A. McCullen, author and landscape historian, who researched and curated the Phoenix Park element of the exhibition. For his meticulous eye for detail and flair, thanks to Steven McNamara for the exhibition design. To Jurga Rakauskaite, thanks for her assistance with the graphic design, and to Motoko Fujita for her photography.

I would like to acknowledge all those institutions, foundations, private collections and individuals who provided images, artefacts and material for this magnificent exhibition.

Thanks to the hardworking exhibition team in Phoenix Park, Farmleigh and National Historic Properties, led by Margaret Gormley, Chief Park Superintendent, for their various roles in this exhibition. Special thanks to Bridgeen Kelly, Paul McDonnell, Maurice Cleary, Raychel Coyle, Pat Blair, Niamh Guihen, Norma Shine, Brian Caffrey, Nicola Meneses, Margaret McGuirk, Linda Moran, Irene Barry, Brian Sweeney, Nuala Canney, Angela Cassidy, Gerry Donoghue, Grace Marshall and Ben Fay.

Thanks also to Maurice Buckley, Chairman of the Office of Public Works, and Rosemary Collier, Director of National Historic Properties; your support is greatly acknowledged. I am extremely grateful to Jacquie Moore, art advisor, and to Barry Nangle, Ciaran Conroy and Niall McKenna in the Press Office.

For their attention to detail, commitment and perseverance, I would like to sincerely thank the team behind the production of the catalogue: Paul Martin, designer; Marie Harpur, catalogue co-ordinator, Elizabeth Mayes, text editor and Printrun, printers.

John McMahon
Commissioner
The Office of Public Works

PARKS: OUR SHARED HERITAGE

'The Royal Parks of London and Phoenix Park in Dublin share a long and distinguished heritage.'

1 FORMATION AND DEVELOPMENT

The Royal Parks of London and Phoenix Park in Dublin share a long and distinguished heritage as well as many other similarities. This is unsurprising, because all these magnificent public parks began as royal hunting grounds and were developed over many centuries by the same people.

Greenwich Park is the oldest of the parks and is the birthplace of Henry VIII (1491-1547), who went on to create Hyde Park, St James's Park and Regent's Park to indulge his love of hunting. Richmond Park was enclosed by Charles I and Green Park by his son, Charles II, also for hunting. Bushy Park was formed by Cardinal Wolsey, but soon gifted to Henry VIII to be populated with deer.

During Oliver Cromwell's protectorate (1653-1658), the London parks passed to the Government and the City of London. Many of the parks suffered – Regent's Park was stripped of trees to pay debts and Hyde Park closed to the public. The restoration of the monarchy under Charles II in 1660 brought the parks back into royal stewardship, with renewed investment, protection and gradual opening to public use. For centuries, the stewardship of the monarchy protected these much loved open spaces from development, as London grew from a small town east of St James's Park to a large city surrounding all the parks. When formed, Bushy Park was ten miles from London. Now it is surrounded by London's suburbia.

Phoenix Park was first mentioned officially in a King's letter of December 1st 1662. Established by James Butler, Duke of Ormonde, Lord Lieutenant of Ireland, on behalf of Charles II, as a royal deer park, it originally included the demesne of Kilmainham Priory south of the river Liffey and covered an area of approximately 2,000 acres which was later reduced to 1752 acres with the building of the Royal Hospital at Kilmainham (1680 -1684). The Park which had been enclosed with a stone wall had its boundaries adjusted and modified accordingly.

Though the boundaries remained mostly constant, the landscapes have undergone considerable development in the gradual transition from royal chases to public parks. While both uses are recreational, it is ironic that enclosure for personal enjoyment now brings great pleasure to so many.

During the years of royal patronage many major projects were undertaken in the London parks. The 19km Longford river which flows through Bushy Park was, on the request of Charles I, dug by hand over the course of nine months in 1638/39 to carry water to Hampton Court. The Serpentine Lake in Hyde Park was created for Queen Caroline, wife of George II, by damming the river Westbourne.

Regent's Park only took its current form when John Nash attempted transformation with plans for 56 villas. Though only eight were ever built, the circular shape, lake and canals of the park owe their existence to Nash's ambitious scheme. Primrose Hill was added in 1841 by purchase from Eton College to give the people of north London more outdoor recreation space.

In the beginning of the 19th century Phoenix Park was neglected – the roads were in bad condition, the landscape poorly drained and the majority of the trees old and in a state of decay. Under the management of the Commissioners for Woods & Forests from the 1830s, and the employment of the renowned architect and landscape architect Decimus Burton, major landscape and infrastructural works were undertaken.

These included landscape restoration, the building of new gatelodges, tree planting, the construction of new roads and the realignment of others, as well as the restoration of the Park's boundary wall. Burton also supplied plans for the layout of the Royal Zoological Gardens (now Dublin Zoo) in 1832, having previously laid out London Zoo in 1825. He also laid out the promenade grounds in 1840 at the city end of Phoenix Park which later developed into the People's Flower Gardens. A bandstand and a tea kiosk were also erected in an area between the Royal Zoological Gardens and the People's Flower Gardens in the 1890s.

Further Park improvements were undertaken by the Office of Public Works (OPW) from 1860. The Wellington Testimonial was completed and two memorials of considerable artistic merit were erected – one in 1870 commemorating the Earl of Carlisle and the other, an equestrian statue to Field Marshal Viscount Gough, in 1880 – both by the renowned sculptor John Henry Foley. Almost a century later a 120ft high cross of fabricated steel was erected in 1979 to commemorate the visit of Pope John Paul II (St John Paul). A statue of

Seán Heuston, one of the 1916 patriots, was also erected in the People's Flower Gardens.

At the beginning of the 20th century, increasing public access brought many landscape changes in all the parks. Sports pitches and tennis courts appeared in Regent's Park, Hyde Park, Bushy Park and Richmond Park, which also became home to the first public golf course where 'Royalty and artisans are equally welcome'. Ornamental gardens were established together with less attractive, but functional, roads and parking for cars.

Historic buildings like Ashtown Castle and Áras an Uachtaráin, the former Viceregal Lodge, in Phoenix Park, and Kensington Palace and Pembroke Lodge in London, offer increasingly public access, while new buildings like the Dell by the Serpentine continue the long tradition of refreshments, dating back centuries, to the Cake House in Hyde Park. Responsible stewardship has led to evolutionary rather than revolutionary development and one can still sense the essence of the original deer parks when roaming in the tranquil wilderness of these splendid public spaces.

'The long-term vision for Phoenix Park combines its protection, conservation, enjoyment and tranquillity.'

Richard Blome, *A Mapp of ye County of Middlesex with its Hundreds,* 1673

In 1673, London was very small in comparison with the metropolis today. St James's Park was on its western suburb, with Hyde Park nearby and, to the north, Marylebone Park, later to become Regent's Park and Primrose Hill. Bushy Park is shown as an enclosure in the depths of the countryside, close to Hampton Court. 'Hundreds' are sub-divisions of a county.

Today all of these parks are surrounded by the sprawl of London. Fortunately, through good stewardship they have survived largely intact as open spaces for all to enjoy.

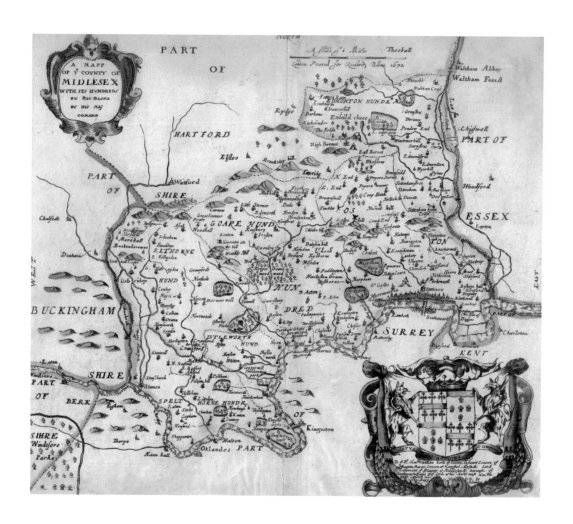

17

John Speed, *Surrey Described and Divided into Hundreds,* 1610

Richmond Park is shown just east of Kingston, but unnamed. Greenwich Park is shown just left of the vignette top right. The vignette top left is of Richmond Palace, built by Henry VII and a favourite residence of Queen Elizabeth I. Only a very small part of the palace remains but its greatest legacy is Richmond Park.

Charles I brought his court to Richmond Palace in 1625 to escape the plague in London. As one 'excessively fond of hunting', he found the existing deer park inadequate and so formed the much larger New Park, later known as Richmond Park.

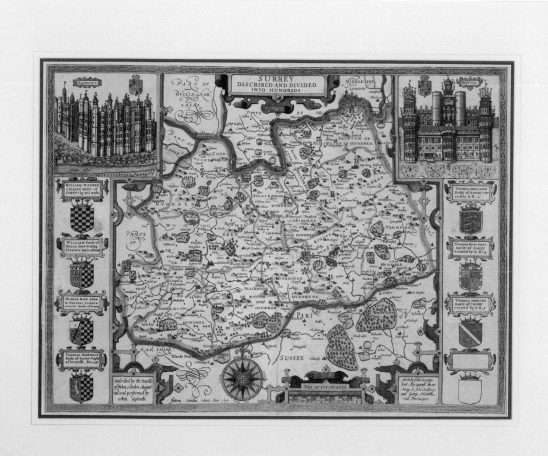

Robert Girdler, *The Parish of Kilmainham, in the County of Dublin.* Down Survey Map, 1650

This map shows the nucleus of the lands which eventually formed the Phoenix Park including the Crown lands of Kilmainham which were located on both sides of the river Liffey. Also included is the 'Newtowne and Phoenix Townland' which shows the important houses of the area such as Newtowne and Phoenix Houses as well as the town of Kilmainham and the village of Chapelizod. Phoenix House was occupied by Henry Cromwell (son of Oliver) for a time.

In 1174 Richard Strongbow, Earl of Pembroke, granted these lands to the Knights Hospitallers of St John of Jerusalem. In 1542 the lands reverted to the Crown when they were confiscated by Henry VIII, only to be restored to the Knights by Queen Mary in 1557. They reverted to the Crown yet again the following year when Elizabeth I succeeded to the throne.

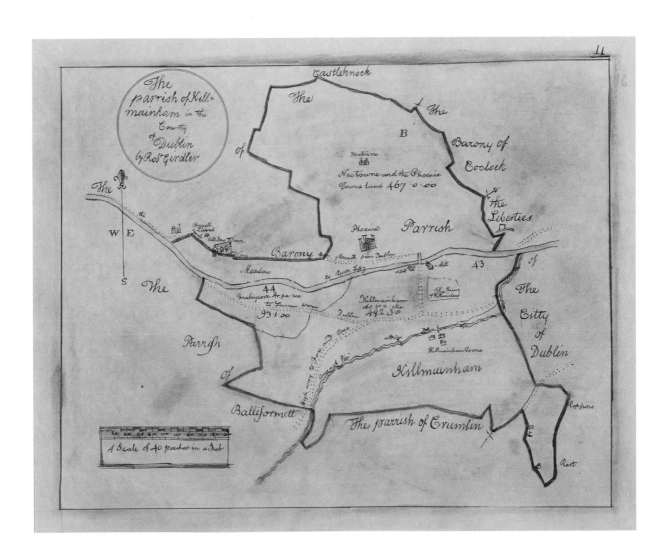

The parrish of Kill=
mainham in the
County
of Dublin
by Robt Girdler

Castleknock

The

The

Barony of
Coolock

B

the
Liberties

Newtowne

Newtowne and the Phoenix
Towne Land 467 : 0 : 00

Of

Parrish

Phoenix

The

N

W — E

S

Barony

The

Meadow

44
Inchycore Arpa me
to Luan hom
93 : 00

Monath from Dublin

the River Liffy

Mill

Mill

43

The

Citty

of

Dublin

Killmainham
Arpa me
4423 0

Dublin

The Kings
F Rt Rhandon

The

Parrish

Killmainham Towne

Killmainham

Of

Balliformett

High way to

The parrish of Crumlin

Roppers

Rest

John Michael Wright (1617-1694) (in the style of), *James Butler, 1st Duke of Ormonde*

Phoenix Park was established as a royal deer park by James Butler, first Duke of Ormonde, one of Ireland's most illustrious Viceroys, on behalf of Charles II. Ormonde had been exiled with the King in France and on his return to Ireland was determined to improve the splendour of the city of Dublin.

The Park originally included the demesne of Kilmainham Priory south of the river Liffey and covered an area of approximately 2,000 acres but was reduced to its present size of 1752 acres with the building of the Royal Hospital at Kilmainham. The building of the hospital in 1680 was one of Ormonde's benevolent projects for the care of old soldiers.

A resolution for forming a royal deer park on the Kilmainham lands was first mooted around 1600 during the reign of Queen Elizabeth I but nothing appears to have happened. Another attempt was made in 1623 to enclose 'His Majesty's [King James I] park near Dublin' for breeding deer and maintaining game.

Approximately forty years later, Phoenix Park is mentioned officially in a King's letter dated 1 December 1662, a few months after the Duke of Ormonde had arrived in Ireland as the new Lord Lieutenant.

Thomas Taylor, *A Survey of the Park of Newtowne and Kilmainham left out of the Phoenix Park, Dublin,* 1671

Since the original purpose of acquiring these lands was the creation of a deer park, it was necessary to enclose them to contain the deer. The mammoth task of building the Park wall fell to William Dodson. The wall, five and three-fifths statute miles long, was poorly constructed and in November 1664 a mile length of the wall had to be pulled down. This was hardly surprising since it was a dry wall construction without mortar. Somewhat surprisingly, Dodson successfully negotiated £100 annually for a period of seven years for the repair of the newly erected wall. An enquiry in 1667 found the wall to have been so badly constructed that two-thirds of it had to be rebuilt. Slightly more than £6,000 had been spent on building it.

With the reduction in the size of the Park, a new wall was constructed on the northern side of the river Liffey and completed in 1682. The new wall of stone and lime, which was eight feet high, extended from the Parkgate Street entrance to Chapelizod. Extensive rebuilding and repairs were further carried out by Decimus Burton in the 1840s.

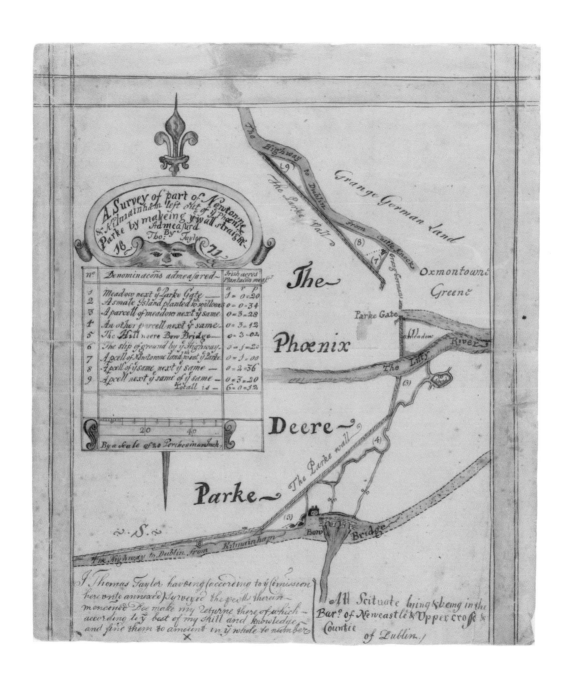

William III, *Direction to increase deer stock in Hide Park,* 1699

To this day the deer in the royal parks of London remain the property of the sovereign. In times past, sovereigns took great interest in the deer, issuing clear directions to the rangers managing the parks, as the words of King William III show:

> 'We do intend to increase the stock of Deer in Our Park, called Hide Park...and We do hereby direct that there be a restraint upon the said Park for this Buck or Doe Season, so as that no Deer be kill'd there except by Our particular Warrant....'

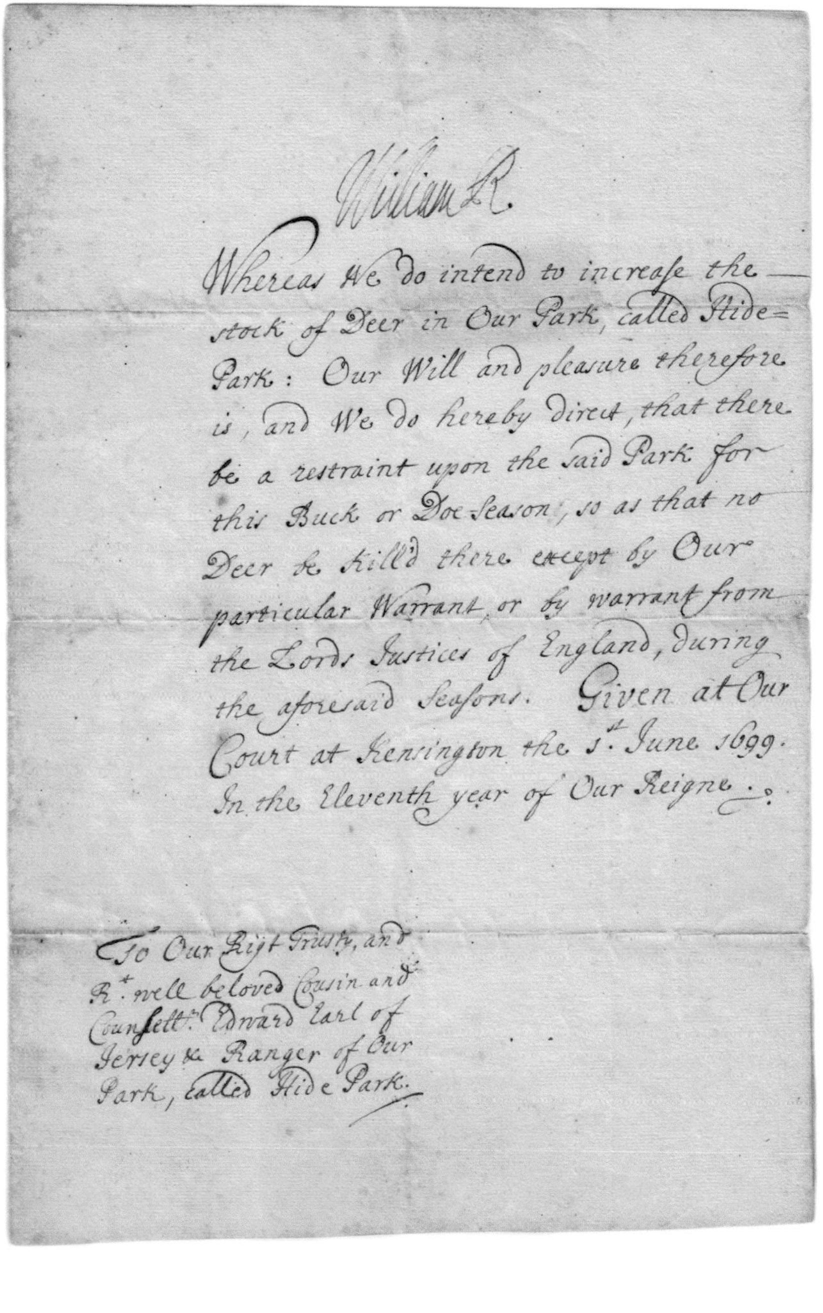

William R.

Whereas We do intend to increase the stock of Deer in Our Park, called Hide=Park: Our Will and pleasure therefore is, and We do hereby direct, that there be a restraint upon the said Park for this Buck or Doe Season, so as that no Deer be kill'd there except by Our particular Warrant, or by warrant from the Lords Justices of England, during the aforesaid Seasons. Given at Our Court at Kensington the 5th June 1699. In the Eleventh year of Our Reigne.

To Our Right Trusty, and
Rt well beloved Cousin and
Counsellr Edward Earl of
Jersey &c Ranger of Our
Park, called Hide Park.

27

Stephen Slaughter, *Philip Dormer Stanhope, 4th Earl of Chesterfield (Lord Lieutenant of Ireland 1745-1746)*, 1746

The Earl of Chesterfield is credited with carrying out extensive works, or at least initiating them, during his term as Lord Lieutenant of Ireland and, more importantly, with facilitating the citizens of Dublin by forming the main road through the Park, still referred to as Chesterfield Road. The opening of the Park to all the people is also attributed to him even though it was already frequented by the nobility in 1731. It appears that only the aristocracy were allowed access to the Park at that time.

With the erection of the Phoenix Column by the Earl of Chesterfield at his own expense in 1747 it became normal for the beaux and belles of society to promenade around the Column on Sunday mornings. In the 1750s only the carriages of persons of distinction were admitted to the Phoenix Park in the fawning season, on orders signed by the Park bailiff.

Chesterfield had humanitarian ideals and initiated schemes for the employment of the poor, one of which was tree planting in Phoenix Park.

29

Leonard Knyff (engraved by Johannes Kip), *New Park,* 1709

Part of Richmond Park was leased in 1686 to Lawrence Hyde, Earl of Rochester. By 1692 Rochester had replaced Petersham Lodge with the splendid mansion, New Park, shown here. It was destroyed by fire less than thirty years later, in 1721. A new Petersham Lodge was built for William, Earl of Harrington in 1733. This, too, was demolished and the land reverted to parkland in 1835.

A children's playground now occupies the site and a few cedar trees are the only reminder of its existence.

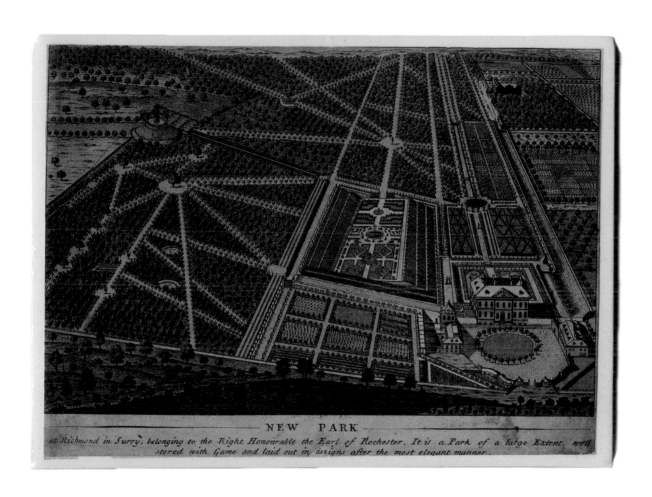

NEW PARK

at Richmond in Surry, belonging to the Right Honourable the Earl of Rochester. It is a Park of a large Extent, well stored with Game and laid out in designs after the most elegant manner.

A print from the book, *Two Historical Accounts ... of New Forest and Richmond New Park,* 1751

In 1751, Princess Amelia (1711-1786), second daughter of George II, became Ranger and limited further access to Richmond Park. On Ascension Day, 16 May, a party of Richmond parish officials taking part in the tradition of Beating the Parish Bounds entered the park through a breach in the wall. Whether this was an existing or a 'created' breach is unknown.

The book was addressed to the 'Citizens of London' and describes local opposition to the enclosure of the park by Charles I and subsequent access restrictions, causing 'the People loudly to complain'. It ends with the exhortation, 'All true lovers of old British liberty will join in supporting such a cause'.

Ironically, enclosure saved the park from being engulfed by suburban development and led to the creation of a much loved public park.

33

Thomas Stewart, *John Lewis of Richmond,* 1793

A humble but brave brewer, John Lewis, took up the cause of access to Richmond Park with two legal actions. The first failed but the second achieved access by ladderstiles at Sheen and Ham gates. Their opening in 1758 was attended by 'a vast concourse of people from all the neighbouring villages'.

John Lewis died poor in 1792, but is commemorated by an epitaph in Richmond parish church and a plaque on Sheen Gate.

James Asser, *A drawing of His Majesty's Park The Phenix in the Kingdom of Ireland, Dublin, c.1775*

This beautifully executed map provides a valuable and detailed account of both the landscape and architecture of the Park including its many military establishments such as the enormous Lord Wharton's Fortification and the Magazine Fort. Official residences belonging to the Park keepers, Park rangers, gatekeepers and others associated with Park management are also highlighted as well as institutions such as the Royal Hibernian Military School and the plot of ground referred to as the Fifteen Acres, which was a military enclosure for training purposes.

Two other interesting landscape features are shown on the map – one is a mound-like feature between Castleknock Gate and Ashtown Gate in the north-eastern area of the Park and the other is a landscape feature known as 'The Wilderness' in the Viceregal demesne (now Áras an Uachtaráin). The former may have been a 'mount' which acted as a focal point within a designed landscape for viewing the local landscape and was a feature of historic landscapes.

The term 'wilderness' historically was used to describe a designed wood or grove with paths cut through it. Its shape was usually regular and in essence it was an attractive area in which to wander and pause. Some of the best examples of this formal French-style 17th-century landscape feature are at Kilruddery in County Wicklow, Antrim Castle and Ham House in Surrey.

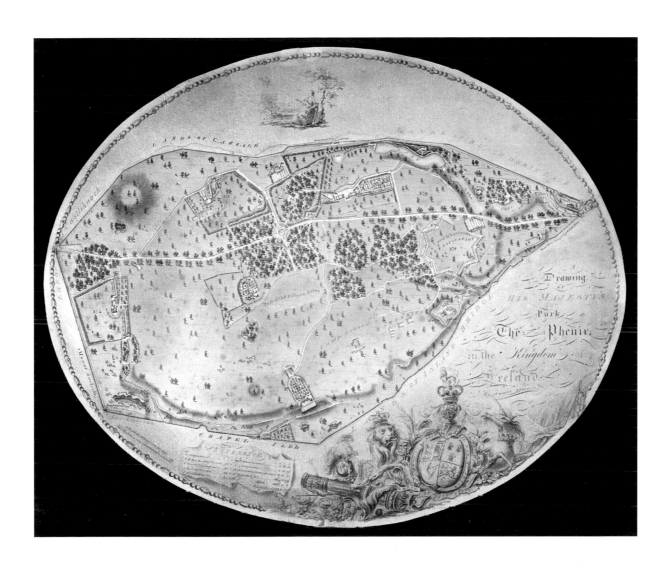

John Henry Campbell (attrib.), *The Under-secretary's Lodge, Phoenix Park, Dublin, c.1755-1828*

The Under-secretary's lodge was the third and final residence purchased by the Government in 1664, along with the lands at Ashtown which included Ashtown Castle. This eventually became the residence of the Ranger of the Park and in time that of the Under-secretary. It also was the residence of the Keeper of the Ashtown Walk from early in the Park's history.

About the year 1760 the tower of the castle, which may date from the 1430s, was incorporated into a new house that became known as Ashtown Lodge. The tower is clearly illustrated on the left side of Campbell's painting.

Ashtown Lodge was the home of successive under-secretaries for Ireland until Irish independence and was occupied by distinguished holders of the office such as Thomas Drummond who died in 1840 and was the last person to hold the combined offices of Park Ranger and Under-secretary. Drummond worked tirelessly on behalf of the Irish people. His predecessor was Lieutenant-Colonel Sir William Gosset, who was Under-secretary from 1831 to 1835. William Gregory has the distinction of being the longest serving Under-secretary for Ireland, from 1812 to 1830.

From the 1930s Ashtown Lodge and demesne was occupied by various Papal Nuncios before being vacated in 1978 and subsequently developed as the Phoenix Park Visitor Centre in the early 1990s.

Pembroke Lodge, Richmond Park, 1847

This idyllic rural scene is a snapshot of just one era. The lodge began life as a mole-catcher's cottage, and was subsequently extended to 'Hill Lodge' for a gamekeeper, John Trage. Between 1785 and 1796, Sir John Soane oversaw further enlargement for the eponymous Countess of Pembroke. More grace-and-favour aristocratic occupants succeeded the Countess until the lodge was requisitioned in 1941 by the Phantom Squad, a highly secret and successful military intelligence unit.

In 1952 the lodge was brutally converted to flats for park staff. Bertrand Russell, a former resident, remarked pithily 'the Government are doing great works, all bad'. From 1974 to 1996, the lodge lay derelict and decaying while a plan for its sale as a private residence was hotly debated.

Between 1997 and 2007, it was restored by the Hearsum family and opened to the public, providing refreshments, conveniences, a trial visitor centre and wedding venues that generate much income for the Park and a temporary home for the Hearsum Collection.

PEMBROKE LODGE, RICHMOND PARK.

41

Anon., *The Viceregal Lodge...Deer grazing on Front Lawn, The Phoenix Park Dublin,* **unsigned and undated**

This watercolour illustrates a pastoral setting for the Viceregal Lodge and can be dated before 1835. A few years later, Decimus Burton, the famous English architect, in collaboration with Lady Normanby (wife of the then Lord Lieutenant) decided on a more formal setting with the enclosure of the 'front lawn' with a raised balustraded terrace overlooking a formal parterre which embodies two Celtic crosses which still survive.

The original house was built in 1751 by Nathaniel Clements when he was Chief Ranger of Phoenix Park. The core structure of that house is virtually intact within the building which subsequently became the official residence of Viceroys, Lord Lieutenants and Governors General between 1782 and 1932.

King George IV was the first monarch to stay at the Viceregal Lodge, in 1821, and Queen Victoria stayed here on four occasions during her visits to Ireland.

It is now known as Áras an Uachtaráin (the President's House) and occupied by the President of Ireland. Official state business takes place here and it is increasingly open to the public.

The Chestnuts and the Diana Fountain, Bushy Park, 1876

Although not apparent from this romantic print, Chestnut Avenue in Bushy Park is strikingly similar to Chesterfield Road in Phoenix Park. Chestnut trees are significant landscape features for both parks and their chestnuts are an important part of the deer's diet.

The Diana Fountain was designed in 1637 by Hubert Le Sueur at the request of King Charles I for his wife, Henrietta Maria. This bronze statue of a goddess (sometimes described as Arethusa) is set on a marble and stone fountain, surrounded by bronze figures of four boys, four water nymphs and four shells. In 1713, the fountain with its statue was moved to Bushy Park, to be the principal feature of Chestnut Avenue, where it still stands today.

The Chestnuts in Bushey Park.

45

Unknown artist, 18th century, *St James's Park, taken near the stable yard, 1794*

St James's Palace is depicted to the left, with deer, and Westminster Cathedral to the right.

Built between 1531 and 1536 for Henry VIII on the site of a leper hospital, the palace, which stands on the north side of the Mall, has been home to many monarchs and hosted momentous events, including the signing of the first treaty to establish the United Nations on 12 June 1941.

Charles II commissioned many landscaping works, including the digging by 300 men of the rectangular canal, now reshaped to organic form. The King granted some public access and 'oft mingled with his subjects'.

Visitors to the Mall in the 17th and 18th centuries varied from promenaders to prostitutes. As transport developed so did the Mall. A pedestrian path surfaced with cockleshells was improved for use by carriages and eventually surfaced with tarmac for motor traffic. All the paraphernalia for traffic – signals, bollards and lights – are removable for ceremonials.

The Mall is known worldwide for royal ceremonials, state visits, Olympic games and even the occasional street party.

A View of St. JAMES'S PARK, taken near the Stable Yard.
Comprehending St. James's Palace, Westminster Abby, Whitehall &c.

Vue du Parc de St. JACQUES, prise du Cour d'Etable.
D'ou l'on decouvre le Palais Royal de St. Jacques l'Abbaie de Westminstre, Whitehall, &c.

Re-Published 12. May 1794 by LAURIE & WHITTLE, 53 Fleet Street London.

Thomas Dugdale, *The Queen's Palace, Pimlico, Middlesex, c.*1842

Queen Anne was not pleased by the construction of Buckingham House at the western end of the Mall in 1703; she thought it was inappropriately dominant within St James's Park. George III, desiring a residence in the city, purchased the house from its owner, the Duke of Buckingham, a friend of the Queen, in 1761.

There were many subsequent improvements, including the Marble Arch, designed by John Nash in 1827 to be the state entrance to Buckingham Palace. In 1847, the arch was dismantled and rebuilt by Thomas Cubitt as a ceremonial entrance at the north-east corner of Hyde Park.

This enabled the construction of the façade we see today. Designed by Nash in his autumn years, it is both grand and world famous.

Sir Edwin Landseer, RA (attrib.), *A View In Richmond Park,* 1844

This charming oil painting epitomises Richmond Park. As in Phoenix Park, the essence of the park is characterised by deer and ancient oaks, some of which are 800 years old.

The bloodlines of the herd date back to enclosure in 1637, with the occasional introduction of stags and bucks to strengthen the gene pool.

Ancient oaks contain exceptional biodiversity, including nationally endangered species of fungi, and nationally scarce invertebrates such as the cardinal click beetle and the stag beetle. The team at the Royal Parks are acknowledged as leading experts in their care.

Landseer was renowned for his paintings of deer and one of the finest examples can be seen at Farmleigh. He was a regular visitor to Richmond, home of his loyal patrons the Duke and Duchess of Abercorn.

Decimus Burton, *Ashtown Gatelodge, Phoenix Park… No.2 design for the proposed lodge, Dublin,* 1839

This coloured architectural drawing is one of a large number of drawings which illustrate not only proposals for the Park's lodges but also for landscape improvements and infrastructural works such as roads and bridges.

Burton's use of red brick for external cladding at the Ashtown Lodges appears to be unique as far as his gatelodges are concerned, either in the Phoenix Park or in England.

With the appointment of Decimus Burton as landscape architect for Phoenix Park, under the Commissioners for Woods and Forests, major landscape and architectural works took place between 1832 and 1849. Burton's reputation had already been well established with the Commissioners through his works on the Royal Parks in London, including his designs for lodges and gateways in Hyde Park which he provided in 1825.

A year later he provided designs for zoological gardens in Regent's Park for the newly founded Zoological Society of London. This probably influenced the Royal Dublin Zoological Society to engage him as their architect for the zoological gardens in Phoenix Park, for which he submitted a report and plans in October 1832.

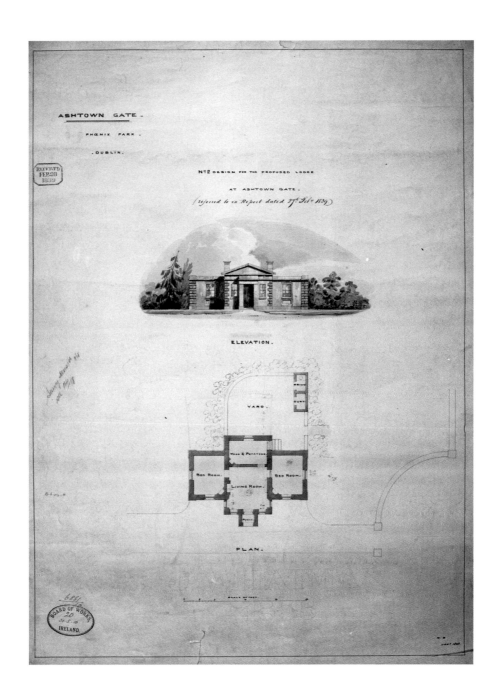

ASHTOWN GATE.

PHŒNIX PARK.

DUBLIN.

Nº 2 DESIGN FOR THE PROPOSED LODGE

AT ASHTOWN GATE.

(referred to in Report dated 27th Feby 1839)

ELEVATION.

PLAN.

The Zoological Gardens, Regent's Park, c.1851

Another feature common to the parks of London and Dublin is that both have devoted significant areas to zoos. In both cases the architect was Decimus Burton, so called because he was the tenth son.

London Zoo is the world's oldest scientific zoo, opened as a collection for scientific study on 27 April 1828. It was eventually opened to the public in 1847. Today it houses a collection of 756 species of animals, with 17,480 specimens, making it one of the largest collections in the United Kingdom.

London Zoo also opened the first reptile house (1849), the first public aquarium (1853), the first insect house (1881) and the first children's zoo (1938).

55

Captain Richard Cobham, Sworn witness statement, manuscript, 1700

Despite various attempts to ban the practice, duelling remained popular among gentlemen, fuelled by testosterone and a perceived need to display courage, in the 17th and 18th centuries. If a gentleman considered his honour had been impugned by another, he would 'demand satisfaction', meaning a one-to-one fight with swords or pistols before witnesses.

Public places like Hyde Park were favoured locations for these encounters, which were often fatal. The manuscript above shows the sworn statement of a Captain Richard Cobham who was witness when Captain Robert Swift killed Colonel Edward Dutton Colt in Hyde Park in December 1700.

Maddx
+
Wittm. \}61

The Examination of Capt Richard
Cobham taken upon oath before me Rodney
ffane Esqr one of his Majesties Justices
of the Peace of the County and Liberty
aforesaid who saith that on the Seventh
day of December 1700 about eleven a clock in
the morning he this deponent saw Collonel Edward
Dutton Colt and Captn Robert Swift with their
Swords drawn in Hide Park and that the said
Captn Robert Swift did there wound the said
Coll: Edward Dutton Colt whilst he the said Swift
did hold the blade of the said Coll: Colts sword in
his hand of which wound the said Collonel
Colt did instantly die.

Rich Cobham

Jurat coram me
7o die x bris
Rodney ffane.

Anon., *The Royal Palace of Kensington,* 1745-1760

King William and Queen Mary, who reigned jointly from 1689 to 1702, asked Christopher Wren, the architect of St Paul's Cathedral, to turn Nottingham House into a palace. The clerk of works, Nicholas Hawksmoor, was told to do the job quickly and cheaply. It was built in six months with brickwork rather than stone and the King and Queen took up residence on Christmas Eve 1689. They opened the gardens to the public on Sundays, when they went to Richmond.

Over the next few years, a gallery, the Queen's apartments and a new entrance were added. Queen Mary had little time to enjoy her new palace, however, as she died from smallpox in 1694. In 1702, King William died at Kensington Palace from complications of a broken collar bone caused when his horse Sorrel stumbled on a molehill.

Queen Victoria was born at Kensington Palace and lived there until 1837. Diana, Princess of Wales had an apartment at the palace from 1981 to 1997.

The Royal Palace of Kensington.   Le Palais Royale de Kensington.

Published by J. Watts, N°. Fleet Street, London.

Entrance Tokens to Richmond Park, 18th century

When Richmond Park was a private royal hunting ground, the public were excluded for reasons of royal privacy and safety.

Nonetheless, access was granted to a privileged few on production of a token or 'card of admission'. These state that New Park, now known as Richmond Park, was preceded by four earlier and smaller deer parks.

'Since the 17th century the Trooping of the Colour in military splendour has taken place in St James's Park to mark the Sovereign's official birthday.'

2   CELEBRATION AND COMMEMORATION

For hundreds of years the Royal Parks have been at the heart of national celebrations and commemorations, from the jousts and revelries enjoyed by Henry VIII in Greenwich Park to Elizabeth II's Silver, Golden and Diamond Jubilees at Hyde, Bushy and Richmond Park respectively.

The Phoenix Park, too, has hosted numerous national and international events which have attracted large numbers of visitors from home and abroad.

Fireworks displays were a popular means of celebration to mark peace treaties and other major events and these were popular not only in Phoenix Park and London's Royal Parks but also in other European capitals and cities. Such celebrations do not always go to plan, however. Green Park was home to the Temple of Peace and the Temple of Concord, but both were soon destroyed by fireworks during festivities in the Park. The first, erected to celebrate the end of the War of Austrian Succession, exploded in a firework display in 1749, and the second in 1814 during the Prince Regent's Gala. In 1814 several spectators lost their lives in St James's Park when the seven-storey Chinese Pagoda was set alight by fireworks.

One of the earliest forms of celebration in Phoenix Park was the firing of cannon from the Salute Battery which occupied a vantage point over the city. Cannon salutes were fired to celebrate coronations, the King's accession, his birthdays and other significant events. Royal marriages and births were also celebrated and royal visits attracted large numbers of spectators. Because of the dangers of the cannon misfiring, a bell was rung before firing to summon a surgeon to attend.

Some celebrations have been fantastically elaborate, such as the fireworks and a naval re-enactment in Hyde Park to mark the end of the Napoleonic wars. Others were fantastically bizarre, like the floating of two elephants down the Serpentine during the celebration of the accession of George IV.

Other celebrations were awe-inspiring, such as the Great Exhibition of 1851 in Hyde Park. Open for nine months, the Great Exhibition was first in a craze of World Fairs displaying and celebrating modern technology. Housed in the Crystal Palace, a cast iron and glass structure of some 92,000 square metres, the Exhibition attracted the equivalent of a third of the population of England at the time and generated a £18m surplus in today's money. This was used to found the Victoria & Albert Museum, the Science Museum and the Natural History Museum in South Kensington as well as an educational grant for industrial research which continues to this day.

The parks have also hosted many long-standing spectacular and popular annual celebrations. Since the 17th century the Trooping of the Colour in military splendour has taken place in St James's Park to mark the sovereign's official birthday, and since the reign of Queen Victoria, Bushy Park has hosted the annual Chestnut Sunday festivities, celebrating the magnificent blossom on the horse chestnut trees.

In all the parks a number of diverse commemorative testimonials and monuments were erected, primarily dedicated to persons associated with the parks or events associated with those persons. In the Royal Parks more than fifty memorials have been installed, from the quaint Peter Pan statue in Kensington Gardens, and the unusual dogs' cemetery, to the fountain in memory of Diana, Princess of Wales, in Hyde Park.

In Phoenix Park the oldest of these monuments is the Phoenix Column, erected in 1747 by the fourth Earl of Chesterfield when Lord Lieutenant of Ireland. Statues were also erected in the 19th century to commemorate the seventh Earl of Carlisle, who served two terms as Lord Lieutenant of Ireland and was also associated with the development of the People's Flower Gardens, while the monument to Field Marshal Viscount Gough, unveiled in the Park in 1880, is considered one of Ireland's finest equestrian statues, both of which are by John Henry Foley. Queen Victoria considered Foley very talented and rewarded him handsomely from her private purse for his execution of the Prince Albert Memorial located in Hyde Park.

The Papal Cross marks the site on the Fifteen Acres, a former military parade ground in Phoenix Park, where in 1979 the Pope celebrated a mass which was attended by more than a million people. The occasion was reminiscent of previous religious events held in the Park which included the centenary of Catholic Emancipation (1929) and the Eucharistic Congress (1932).

The Royal Parks and Phoenix Park contain many memorials to Arthur Wellesley, first Duke of Wellington (1769-1852), who is an exemplar of our shared heritage. The most celebrated is the Wellington Testimonial, an obelisk erected in Phoenix Park in 1817 to celebrate the Duke of Wellington's illustrious military career.

Wellington was born, educated and married in Ireland, becoming a highly respected general and twice Prime Minister of Great Britain. He had been aide-de-camp to two Lord Lieutenants and Chief Secretary for Ireland, as well as Ranger for the Royal Parks.

The ceremonial trees within the Phoenix Park are its most celebrated arboricultural feature. The first recorded ceremonial planting is that of an English Oak (Quercus robur) planted by Queen Victoria in September 1853. Numerous other plantings have taken place since then and the tradition of ceremonial tree planting by visiting heads of State in the grounds of Áras an Uachtaráin still continues.

'Wellington was born, educated and married in Ireland, becoming a highly respected General and twice Prime Minister of Great Britain.'

Francis Jukes, *The Salute Battery, Phoenix Park,* 1795

One of the earliest forms of celebration in Phoenix Park was the firing of cannon from the Salute Battery, on ceremonial occasions rather than for defensive purposes. Cannon salutes took place to celebrate events such as coronations, the King's accession and King William's birthday. Royal marriages and births were also celebrated.

The small military installation known as the Salute Battery occupied a vantage point overlooking the city and dates to around 1710. This is one of a series of engravings by Francis Jukes (1745-1812) that show different angles of the structure.

The firing of cannon was a risky and dangerous business for those involved as serious injuries could take place if cannons misfired. It was customary for a bell to be rung before firing to summon a surgeon to attend.

The building fell into disrepair in the early decades of the 19th century and the site was handed over for the erection of the Wellington Testimonial, which commenced in 1817 but was not completed until 1861.

Plate 10

LONDON Pub.^d June 1 1795 by F. Jukes Howland &c.

Dublin

67

The Temple of Peace in the Green Park, 1748

This temple commemorated peace after the War of Austrian Succession (1740-1748), which involved most of the European nations. Conceived as an elaborate Doric temple, it was monumental at 410 feet long and 114 feet high. One hundred and twelve musicians and a hundred cannon were synchronised with a spectacular firework display, including an artificial sun that was to burn for four hours. Unsurprisingly, the designer fell ill before completion and his deputy was severely injured.

The opening night on 27 April 1748 began with the War and Peace overture, commissioned from Handel, but just ninety minutes later the structure was destroyed by fire. At a cost of three lives and £90,000, equivalent to over £18m today, this was a very expensive ninety minutes.

69

Anon., *A View in Hyde Park with the Fleet at Anchor on the Serpentine,* **1814**

The view makes an interesting contrast to the blue pedalos seen on the Serpentine today.

This grand 'Naumachia' on the Serpentine was a re-enactment of the Battle of the Nile in 1798 between the English fleet under Admiral Nelson and the French fleet under Admiral Brueys d'Aigalliers. To re-enact such a large naval battle within a comparatively small and shallow lake was a major challenge, but very popular with spectators.

It was the centrepiece of the Jubilee Fair of 1814 held in Hyde Park to commemorate the end of the Napoleonic wars with France.

View in Hyde Park, with the Fleet at Anchor, on the Serpentine River.

Published Aug.ᵗ 10, 1814, by Thoˢ. Palser Surry Side Westᵐ. Bridge

on the occasion of the Visit of the Allied Sovereigns, Emperor of Rustia & Prussia &c &c

JP Neale (engraved by Sands), *The Temple of Concord in the Green Park,* **1814**

The revolving temple was also part of the Jubilee celebrations in 1814 and was revealed to the public after an impressive fireworks display. The Baroque structure was garishly lit and lavishly decorated with patriotic allegorical scenes celebrating 'The Triumph of England under the Regency'. The building was the work of Sir William Congreve, a military officer and Comptroller of the Royal Laboratory at Woolwich.

Henry de Daubrawa (engraved by John Harris), *A View in Hyde Park,* **1845**

This equestrian portrait depicts the elderly Duke of Wellington (1769-1852) riding past the Wellington Monument. The 18-foot high statue of Achilles in honour of the Iron Duke was cast in bronze by Richard Westmacott from cannon captured at the battles of Salamanca, Vittoria, Toulouse and Waterloo. It was the first statue installed in Hyde Park.

Although it was funded by donations of £10,000 from 'The Ladies of England', the nudity of the statue gave offence, despite its well-placed fig leaf.

Anon., *Deer by the Serpentine, c.*1870

In the distance is the Speke Monument, installed in 1866 in Kensington Gardens, a red granite obelisk dedicated to John Hanning Speke, the explorer who discovered Lake Victoria and led expeditions to the source of the Nile.

He died mysteriously in 1864, with some proclaiming accidental death and others suicide. Speke was shot by his own gun the day before he was due to take part in a debate at the Royal Geographical Society about the source of the river Nile. Speke claimed the source was the Rippon Falls, an outflow from Lake Victoria in east Africa. He would have been opposed in the debate by Sir Richard Burton, another explorer, who argued that Speke did not have conclusive evidence for his claim. Speke was eventually vindicated and the Royal Geographical Society stated he had solved 'the problem of all ages'.

The Great Exhibition, 1851

The spectacular exhibition of innovation, industry and art, devised by Prince Albert, husband of Queen Victoria, and covering eighteen acres, was located in the Crystal Palace, a vast structure of cast iron and glass where the Albert Memorial now stands in Hyde Park. It was designed by Joseph Paxton and built with incredible speed in under eight months.

Miles of frontage within the Crystal Palace contained displays from around the world and attracted six million visitors. The Serpentine Bridge, built in 1826, was opened temporarily to carriages for the exhibition but this access became permanent and has gradually become a busy route for through traffic. As ever with parks, what appears to be an innocuous temporary inconvenience can grow to be an unwelcome permanent feature.

The Crystal Palace featured the first public toilet cubicles. The inventor, George Jennings, charged a penny to each visitor, hence the expression 'spend a penny'.

In 1852 the Crystal Palace was moved to the site that bears its name, but was destroyed by fire in 1936.

EXTERIOR OF THE SOUTH FRONT OF THE GREAT EXHIBITION BUILDING.

Robert Home, *Arthur Wellesley, 1st Duke of Wellington,* 1804

The Duke of Wellington, born in Dublin, probably on 1 May 1769, the same year as Napoleon, had many associations with Phoenix Park. He was aide-de-camp to two Lord Lieutenants of Ireland – first to Lord Buckingham and then in 1790 to the Earl of Westmoreland. He was Chief Secretary for Ireland from 1807 to 1809.

Wellington was proud of his Irish heritage. A well-known saying, 'Being born in a stable does not make a man a horse', has been erroneously attributed to him but is now correctly attributed to Daniel O'Connell, who made the remark, which was 'received with great laughter', at a 'Monster Meeting' at Mullaghmast.

As Chief Secretary for Ireland, Wellington administered anti-Catholic laws with mildness and kindness and tried to create a sense of unity and obliterate distinctions between Catholic and Protestant.

He served as Prime Minister of England from January 1828 until November 1830 and also as Ranger of the Royal Parks for a couple of years before his death in 1852 at the age of 83.

The Peace Commemoration, *The Illustrated London News, Supplement,* 7 June 1856

This print illustrates one of the many fireworks displays which celebrated the end of the Crimean War and the signing of the peace treaty in Paris in 1856. It shows the display in Phoenix Park at the Wellington Testimonial with the Royal Hospital Kilmainham in the background.

The Testimonial which was the focal point of the display was erected to commemorate the Duke of Wellington's victories. It was originally marked for St Stephen's Green Park but after objections to its siting there it eventually was located near the main entrance of Phoenix Park. The successful design for the Testimonial was a 220-feet high obelisk (but when built the obelisk would be 15 feet shorter) by Sir Robert Smirke, who was later to become the designer of the British Museum. At the time it was the largest obelisk in the world, and still remains so in Europe.

Traditionally the Wellington Testimonial was a popular spot for large protest gatherings. In 1792 a public meeting was held here attended by 10,000 tradesmen, apprentices and labourers to protest at the proposed introduction of a draconian labour law. A celebrated Fenian amnesty meeting was held here in August 1871. Having been banned and forcefully disbanded, it was the subject of a number of House of Commons debates when it was conceded that public meetings could in future be held in the Phoenix Park.

As a result of this protest, free speech was recognised as the right of every person not only in Phoenix Park but also in other Royal Parks.

THE PEACE COMMEMORATION

AT DUBLIN.—FIREWORKS IN PHŒNIX PARK.—(SEE PAGE 635.)

William Howis, *The Phoenix Column, The Phoenix Park, Dublin,* 1867

This painting of the Phoenix Column and its environs captures the pastoral ambience and leisure activities which took place in the heart of the Park in the latter half of the 19th century. The Column acted as a focal point for people engaged in conversation, dog walking and horse riding.

Also shown are sheep and cattle grazing, with a gentleman on horseback. The Column is protected by an unclimbable iron railing with four lamp standards at each corner to improve visibility. The Phoenix Column has undergone a number of moves and improvements since it was originally erected in 1747 in the centre of the original Chesterfield Road. When Burton realigned the road in the 1840s it was moved to become a more central focal point. The opportunity was also taken then to raise the column on a series of steps to improve its height and make a greater visual impact. It was raised further in the 1860s, surrounded by cast iron railings and with gas lights erected on four columns.

It was relocated yet again in 1929 to a site nearby before being reinstated in 1986 to its position in the centre of Burton's realigned Chesterfield Road.

Lady St Germans Monument, Viceregal Demesne, the Phoenix Park, Dublin, late 19th century

This small, melancholy monument with its inscribed marble plaque is unique in the history of ceremonial tree planting in the Viceregal Demesne and possibly elsewhere.

Shortly before the St Germans family vacated the Viceregal Lodge, trees were planted by the Earl and Lady St Germans. Soon afterwards, both Lady St Germans and the tree she had planted died, which prompted the new Lord Lieutenant, Lord Carlisle, a friend of the St Germans, to erect this unusual monument to commemorate the events.

This bas-relief memorial in Portland stone depicts a tree, with two verses of poetry composed by the Earl himself inscribed on the marble face at its base.

87

The Wellingtonia at Áras an Uachtaráin

The commemorative plaque records that the ceremonial tree planted by Queen Victoria in August 1861 was a Wellingtonia giganteum, named in honour of the Duke of Wellington after it was discovered in California in 1853. A year later, however, it was renamed Washingtonia californica. Although it was given its proper botanical name of Sequoiadendron giganteum or Giant Redwood in 1930, it is still popularly known in England as Wellingtonia.

Since its introduction, this tree has become a popular choice as a ceremonial tree in Ireland and England. Both President John F. Kennedy of the United States of America and President de Valera planted Giant Redwoods at Áras an Uachtaráin on the occasion of the former's state visit to Ireland in 1963.

W.S. Wilkie's gold pen/pencil combination

This gold pen/pencil combination was presented to William Spalding Wilkie, bailiff of Phoenix Park, on the occasion of the ceremonial tree plantings by Queen Victoria and the Prince Consort that took place in August 1861 in the formal gardens at the Viceregal Lodge (now Áras an Uachtaráin). This was possibly the last tree planted by Prince Albert before he died later that year. Sadly, the tree he planted also died some years later.

The pen set is inscribed as follows:

Presented by Queen Victoria to W.S. Wilkie, Phoenix Park, August 26, 1861.

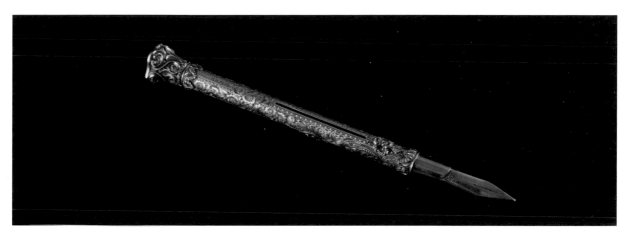

PRESENTED BY
QUEEN VICTORIA
TO W. S. WILKIE
PHŒNIX PARK,   AUGUST 26TH 1861

GH Andrews (engraved by TA Prior), *The Albert Memorial, Hyde Park,* 1869

This very elaborate memorial was commissioned by Queen Victoria in memory of her beloved husband Prince Albert who died of typhoid in 1861. The announcement prompted nationwide mourning and Queen Victoria remained in deep mourning for decades.

The memorial was designed by Sir Gilbert Scott and constructed over ten years at a cost equivalent to £11m today, all met from public subscription. The intricate allegorical figures at each corner of both levels and a highly decorated Gothic canopy contrast vividly with the sombre mourning after his passing.

ALBERT MEMORIAL, HYDE PARK.

Four generations of monarchs: a christening at White Lodge, Richmond Park, 1894

On 23 June 1894, the future Edward VIII was born at White Lodge, the home of his maternal grandparents, the Duke and Duchess of Teck. Queen Victoria attended his christening together with her son, the future Edward VII, and grandson, the future George V, all shown in this photograph.

Queen Victoria wrote in her journal, 'The dear fine baby wearing the Honiton lace robe... [made from her own wedding veil] was brought in and handed to me – I then gave him to the Archbishop and recd him back. The child was very good, I holding the baby in my lap, Bertie and George standing behind me, thus making four generations'.

July 16th 1894.

W. & D. DOWNEY
PHOTOGRAPHERS
COPYRIGHT
57 & 61 EBURY STREET.
LONDON, S.W.

Moving the Wellington Statue, 1883

While the Duke of Wellington was widely respected, this statue of him by Matthew Cotes Wyatt was less popular. Cast in bronze from guns captured at the Battle of Waterloo, it was the largest equestrian statue of the time, at 30 feet high and weighing 40 tons.

The architect of the supporting stone arch, Decimus Burton, thought it disproportionate. Although Burton was not alone in this view, the removal of the statue was considerably delayed until after the death of the Duke of Wellington. In 1883 it was removed to Green Park to be stored until its move to its present location in Aldershot in 1885.

The Coronation of George VI: the King and Queen in the Coronation procession, 1937

Caption on reverse – 'The Royal Coach left for Westminster Abbey for the Coronation of King George and Queen Elizabeth. Picture taken from the roof of Buckingham Palace'.

The central monument on the roundabout was created between 1906 and 1924 by Sir Thomas Brock and is the centrepiece of the Queen Victoria Memorial, which includes much more decorative stonework, concealed in this image by stands.

The Eucharistic Congress, Phoenix Park, 1932

This photograph shows the main altar and the large number of people who attended the 31st Eucharistic Congress in Phoenix Park in June 1932.

Ireland was selected to host the Congress because 1932 was the 1,500th anniversary of the arrival of St Patrick in Ireland. The Eucharistic Congress, one of the largest of the 20th century, was attended by more than a million people, at events which were celebrated in Dublin in June of that year. The world-famous tenor Count John McCormack sang at the closing Mass.

A few years earlier, in 1929, the centenary of Catholic Emancipation in Ireland was held, also in Phoenix Park, attended by 250,000 people. In more recent decades, in September 1979, Phoenix Park was one of a number of venues where Pope John Paul II (now St John Paul) celebrated Mass which was attended by over a million people.

Feeding the Coronation troops, April 1937

Caption on reverse – 'A busy scene in the camp kitchen where food is prepared for 1,600 men, contingents for the troops for the Coronation who are arriving every day at Kensington Gardens'.

As ever, the parks played many roles in major ceremonial events.

Admiralty Arch, Victory Day in London, 1946

Commissioned by King Edward VII as a memorial to Queen Victoria, it was designed by Sir Aston Webb and completed in 1912.

Admiralty Arch plays an important role in many ceremonials. Processions for royal weddings, funerals, coronations and the London 2012 Olympic and Paralympic Games have all passed through the central arch. The outer arches are used for vehicles and pedestrians.

Training horses for crowd control for the Coronation of Queen Elizabeth II, 1953

Caption on reverse – 'A camp has been set up in Hyde Park for the training of horses for the use of VIPs during the Coronation ceremonies. They are being trained by volunteers from the Royal Army Veterinary Corps and the RAF.

RAF Volunteers keep control of the horses as they ride past a party of flag-waving and noise-making children during training in Hyde Park this afternoon. The youngsters were incited to help make a noise and were of course, more than happy to assist'.

The World's Biggest Children's Party, 1979

This was the main event in Britain to celebrate the United Nations International Year of the Child. Around 160,000 children were invited to a two-day party in Hyde Park – the world's biggest children's party. They were welcomed by a 50ft high Kermit the Frog.

Queen Elizabeth II planting a tree at Áras an Uachtárain, 2011

In May 2011, HM Queen Elizabeth II, accompanied by Prince Philip, planted a ceremonial tree in the grounds of Áras an Uachtaráin (formerly the Viceregal Lodge) as part of a four-day official state visit to Ireland. Also present were President Mary McAleese and Robert Norris, head gardener. The tree, an upright English Oak (Quercus robur 'Fastigiata'), continued a long tradition of tree planting by heads of state when visiting Ireland.

During the brief ceremony the Áras Peace Bell was rung by two students – Danny Rea from Northern Ireland and Leah Ennis McLoughlin from Dublin. The Peace Bell was commissioned for the tenth anniversary of the Good Friday Peace Agreement and the oak timber used is symbolic, in that the outer uprights come from Northern Ireland and the Republic of Ireland with the central timber originating from the Phoenix Park.

It was the first visit by a British monarch to the Republic of Ireland since 1911, when Queen Elizabeth's grandfather, King George V, visited, when the entire island of Ireland was still part of the United Kingdom of Great Britain and Ireland.

'For many city dwellers today, the parks represent tranquil sanctuaries and respite from congestion.'

3 MILITARY AND THE WAR YEARS

For many city dwellers today, the parks represent tranquil sanctuaries and respite from congestion. But as large open spaces in London and Dublin, they were enlisted many times throughout the centuries for military planning, drilling, testing and convalescing.

The military use of Phoenix Park in the 18th century not only dominated the landscape with fortifications and military institutions but the Park was also used for military reviews, manoeuvres, encampments and artillery practice.

The Star Fort, commenced by the Duke of Wharton when he was Lord Lieutenant in 1710, was abruptly stopped a year later due to anticipated cost overruns and site unsuitability. A few decades later the Magazine Fort was constructed in a much more strategic location occupying high ground overlooking the river Liffey. This fort has figured prominently in Irish history, having been attacked on two occasions – in April 1916, when some of its munitions were exploded to signal the start of the rebellion, and again in December 1939 when it was raided for guns and ammunition.

Several military institutions were erected in the 18th century. One of these was the Royal Hibernian Military School, built in 1766 and given its royal charter in 1769, for maintaining, educating, and apprenticing the orphans and children of deceased soldiers and those serving abroad. However, during the 19th century a number of military projects were rejected, including a proposal for a national military cemetery and a cavalry barracks.

Drilling and training in the Royal Parks dates back as far as Elizabeth I, who used the Parade Ground in Hyde Park to review her troops. In more modern times the Women's Auxiliary Army drilled in Hyde Park in the 1940s; cavalry charges were practised in Richmond Park; camouflage was tested in Kensington Gardens and Chestnut Avenue in Bushy Park was used as a landing strip for light aircraft.

In Richmond Park, at White Lodge, Lord Nelson drew the battle plans for the Battle of Trafalgar in red wine on a white cloth, while Pembroke Lodge was used during the Second World War as HQ of the Phantom Squad, an elite intelligence unit, and Bushy Park was used by General Dwight Eisenhower to plan Operation Overlord, otherwise known as D-Day.

As unpopulated areas, the parks also offered great opportunity to test inventions and divert enemy planes. During the First World War, Richmond Park was used to trial the ominously named 'death ray' and HG Wells's 'telepherage' system of front line transportation of munitions along a wire. In the Second War, Richmond Park acted as a decoy for German bombers. Pen ponds were drained to prevent their use as a navigation aid and a nearby site was used for Operation Starfish, with large fires set ablaze to divert German bombers from central London.

Both World Wars had an impact on Phoenix Park's landscape and its operations. Trenches were constructed for army training and gardening to supply food. However, the effects of the Second World War were more severe since large areas of the Park were used for allotments for food production. A German bomb dropped on the Phoenix cricket ground caused structural damage to nearby buildings but with no loss of life.

As great expanses of open land, those parts of the parks which avoided military training and testing were turned over to agricultural land in which to 'dig for victory'. Great potato fields covered Richmond and Bushy Parks and allotments and piggeries potted Hyde Park. Considerable areas of Phoenix Park were also devoted to fuel storage which included turf embankments, as well as coal and timber depots, the effects of which lasted long after the war ended.

During the First World War a convalescent home was built for South African troops in Richmond Park and the Upper Lodge in Bushy Park was converted for injured Canadian troops, where Queen Mary visited and ensured entertainment was provided by locals.

Greenwich Park flower gardens were also enlisted into the war effort, with anti-aircraft guns stationed in the flower beds to target German planes using the Thames as a route into London. The tops of the surrounding trees were sawn down to widen the line of fire and their modern truncated shapes remain as one of the few reminders of this great role that the parks played in our military history.

The parks' role did not end with the war. Hyde Park became a great sorting depot for rubble in the reconstruction effort following the Second World War and Regent's Park owes its flat landscape to the huge amounts of war debris deposited on the previously undulating landscape. Phoenix Park is still used by the military for horse riding, sports and fitness training.

'In Richmond Park, at White Lodge, Lord Nelson drew the battle plans for the Battle of Trafalgar in red wine on a white cloth.'

Plan of manoeuvres performed in the Phoenix Park in June 1775, Dublin, ordered by General Irwine

In June 1775 the Dublin garrison, consisting of six regiments of foot and one of horse, performed military manoeuvres which encompassed almost the entire Park.

This map is of great interest to military historians with its detailed battle arrangements, military notes and cartouches (drawings) on the upper right and lower left hand sides of the map. It also clearly depicts the Park's topography, especially along the southern fringes as well as illustrating the Star (Wharton's Fort) and the Magazine Forts.

Numerous reports indicate the scale of the various military activities which were undertaken in the Park. These included military reviews, manoeuvres, artillery practices and encampments and were often reviewed by the Lord Lieutenant. The military reviews frequently coincided with visits from royalty, who took the salute.

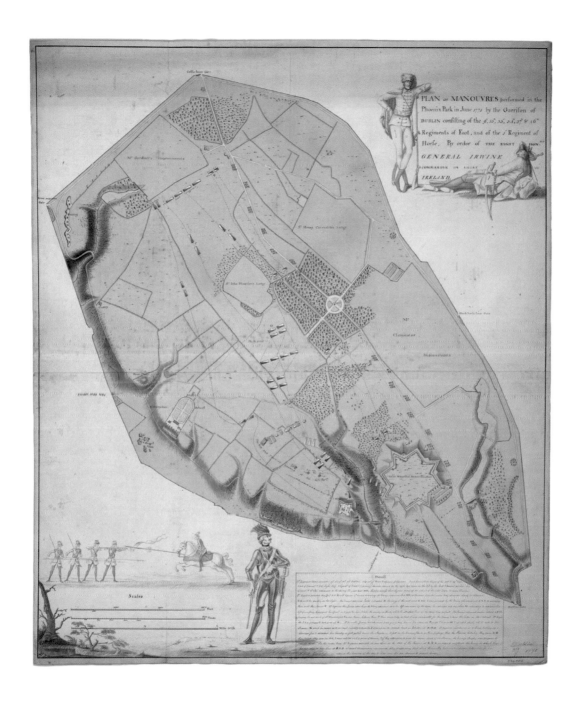

Gabriel Beranger (probable designer), *'The Volunteer Furniture'*, printed by Thomas Harpur of Harpur Mills in Leixlip, late 18th century

This original piece of linen and cotton fabric represents the Provincial Review held in Phoenix Park on 3 June 1782 with Lord Charlemont reviewing the Irish Volunteers of the Province of Leinster.

The fabric illustrates aspects of the military review as well as details of the Park's architecture and landscape. The substantial building shown is the Chief Secretary's Lodge, with an interesting weather vane aloft. The Phoenix Column is shown surrounded by a circular railing which protects the shrubs from deer damage. Evergreen and heavily pruned broad-leaved trees are also shown, although artistic licence has been taken in showing the pruning of the latter.

There are several cameos of social activities depicted on the fabric including a picnic, means of transport and a child falling from a tree.

Thomas Malton, *A Field Day in Hyde Park, 15 May 1789*

A satirical view, perhaps slightly exaggerating the disturbance caused to peaceful park visitors by military practices. Nonetheless, the issues caused by multiple uses of Hyde Park remain to this day. While people still flock to the park seeking tranquillity, frequent military use has been replaced by large concerts and, since 2007, the festive extravaganza, Winter Wonderland.

The Royal Parks work hard to find a balance between the desire of some for tranquillity with the desire of others to attend events and the need for maintenance income.

121

Canaletto (engraved by Thomas Bowles), *A View of the Parade in St James's Park,* **1753**

Originally a tiltyard for jousting during the reign of Henry VIII, this area was used for the birthday celebrations of Elizabeth I. Upon the accession of Charles II it became a mustering and parade area for the Lifeguards.

The tradition of celebrating the sovereign's birthday continues to this day, with the magnificent Trooping the Colour ceremony on Horse Guards Parade. For the rest of the year the area is managed as a public open space, with occasional events such as the 2012 Olympic beach volleyball competition.

Lieutenant P. Cary, *View of the Royal Military Infirmary, Phoenix Park, from the Royal Hospital, Dublin,* probably 1792

The main focus of this painting is the Royal Military Infirmary which overlooks the People's Flower Gardens in Phoenix Park. The Royal Infirmary, or Soldiers' Hospital, was erected in 1786-1788 to the designs of James Gandon, with William Gibson as the executant architect. The Royal Infirmary was subsequently used for both the British and Irish military administrations and is currently used by the Irish Department of Justice.

The proximity of both the river Liffey and the Royal Hospital at Kilmainham is evident in this painting; both of these formed part of the original Phoenix Park before the building of the Royal Hospital in 1680 and the subsequent building of the boundary wall of the Park on the north side of the river.

Also shown is the main entrance to the Park at Parkgate Street with its gated entrance and substantial gatelodge. This was replaced over a four-year period from 1809 to 1813 by an ensemble of lodges, substantial stone gate piers and three pairs of iron gates by the renowned architect Francis Johnston. One of the twin gatelodges was extended to become a police barracks before it was partially demolished in the 20th century.

Richard Earlom (after Robert Smirke), *King George III Reviewing the Volunteer Corps assembled in Hyde Park in honour of his Birthday, 4 June 1799*

In this aquatint we can see that the scale of this review was immense, occupying the entire eastern section of Hyde Park, which is still known today as the Parade Ground.

To the right is the reservoir of the Chelsea Waterworks and the buildings fronting Park Lane, then just a narrow carriageway now a six-lane road, created on former park land.

The fields immediately above the review now contain the buildings of Bayswater and Notting Hill.

A Field Day in the Phoenix Park, 8 May 1843, **print published by W. Kohler, 22 Denmark Street, Dublin**

This amusing print is one of a number of illustrations, paintings and maps which show military reviews in the Phoenix Park.

In 1789 the Irish patriot, Theobald Wolfe Tone, at the age of 17, recorded how he absented himself from school to attend the reviews on the Fifteen Acres which created his 'untamable desire' to be a soldier. Around that time one of the most spectacular recreations for Dubliners was attending the reviews of the Irish militia.

Faulkner's Journal in June 1808 reported that 'The throng which moved along the road to the Phoenix Park on Sunday, invited by the camp and the fineness of the weather, was immense. The camp ground presented a scene of animation and amusement highly gratifying to those who see in the innocent hilarity of their fellow creatures the surest test of their content and happiness'.

The Meteorological Observatory in Phoenix Park, plate from John Cameron, *Meteorological Observations taken during the years 1829 to 1852 at the Ordnance Survey Office,* 1856

The Ordnance Survey Office of Ireland, established in 1825, is located in what was originally Castleknock Lodge (later Mountjoy House), to which numerous individual buildings have since been added. The design of the original lodge is attributed to the Irish architect Edward Lovett Pearce, who also designed a lodge in Richmond Park which was almost certainly for Queen Caroline, who had planned its rebuilding in 1728.

Castleknock Lodge was originally the home of Luke Gardiner who was appointed Keeper of the Castleknock Walk in Phoenix Park in 1728. It later became Mountjoy Barracks (c.1780). As a cavalry barracks, it provided a mounted escort to the Lord Lieutenant, and maintained its military connection when it became the Ordnance Survey headquarters.

Considerable landscape works were undertaken by Decimus Burton on this small demesne where he managed to negotiate a reduction in its original size for the benefit of Park users. By 1853 an extensive designed landscape had developed around the Ordnance Survey Office and it was in the southern section of this landscape that an array of meteorological instruments were located, which has enabled continuous meteorological data to be collected from June 1829 to the present day.

Guards Army manoeuvres in Hyde Park, 1915

Caption on reverse –'Yesterday afternoon, instead of the usual rugby match, the Guards have instructions in Warfare'.

Hyde Park searchlight, 1914

Set incongruously atop the magnificent screen designed by Decimus Burton, this searchlight helped to protect London from Zeppelin bombers.

These large airships were obvious during daylight and vulnerable to anti-aircraft fire, forcing more night raids. Thus searchlights were installed, forcing the Zeppelins to fly at greater heights, reducing their navigational and bombing accuracy. Nonetheless over 500 civilian lives were lost in these raids.

Winston Churchill in a sailor suit, dated 1878, and with his aunt, Lady Leslie, in Dublin 1880

The official residence of the Lord Lieutenant's private secretary was located in a lodge and grounds in the north-west corner of the Viceregal demesne (now Áras an Uachtaráin). The building was originally occupied by a Park Ranger and referred to as the Little Lodge when it was occupied by the Churchills. This lodge, subsequently called Ratra House, became the retirement home of Douglas Hyde, the first President of Ireland.

Lord Randolph Churchill lived here during his term as private secretary (1876-1880) and Winston Churchill's younger brother, John, was born there in 1880. Winston was only two years old when he came to live at the Little Lodge. It is claimed that Winston Churchill often remarked that his fascination for militarism, particularly cavalry, was nurtured from viewing the cavalry from nearby Marlborough Barracks (now known as McKee Barracks) as they paraded on the Fifteen Acres in the Phoenix Park.

Some of his earliest childhood memories hark back to his residency in the Park where he recalled the unveiling of the Gough Statue (1880) by his grandfather, the Duke of Marlborough, Lord Lieutenant at the time; he had also been gifted a drum from T.H. Burke who was Under-secretary for Ireland.

Planned air raid shelter for a million people beneath Hyde Park, 1938

Caption on reverse – 'An artist's illustration of a scheme to build under Hyde Park a great central railway for all the main lines in London. It would not interfere in any way with the present amenities of London's greatest open space, but it would afford shelter for a million people against any sudden air raid. Far more importantly, however, it would enable millions to move out swiftly and safely from the target of bombs to the comparative immunity of the surrounding countryside. It would involve a gigantic development of the City's present traffic system. This is already long overdue. If the risks of heavy casualties and panic among London's population can be reduced, it is believed that Britain could not be defeated in any in European war'.

A bold and ambitious concept that was never built.

PADDINGTON STATION   MARYLEBONE STATION   MARBLE ARCH   EUSTON STATION   KINGS X AND ST. PANCRAS

PARK LANE

EARTH
CLAY

SAND PREPARED TO PREVENT POISON GAS SEEPAGE.

SPECIALLY REINFORCED CONCRETE
60 FT. THICK   PROTECTION FROM 2000 LB.
HIGH EXPLOSIVE BOMBS.

Nº 1 FLOOR

Nº 2 FLOOR

Nº 3 FLOOR

PICCADILLY →

HYDE PARK CORNER STATION.

DECONTAMINATION ROOMS

RAMPS CARRY INTER-FLOOR TRAFFIC.

MADE SURFACE

DIESEL ENGINES ON UPPER FLOOR PROVIDE LIGHT, AND DRIVE AIR-FILTRATION PLANT, OXYGEN RESERVE AND FUEL-OIL STORED BELOW LOWER FLOOR LEVEL.

ADMINISTRATION BLOCK;
C.O's HEADQUARTERS; AIR,
LIGHT, AND TRAFFIC CONTROL
ROOMS: TELEPHONE, RADIO
AND MECHANICAL BUREAUS.

REINFORCED CONCRETE WALLS

TUNNEL TO ⊖

LONDON CLAY

TUNNEL TO WATERLOO

KNIGHTSBRIDGE

ENTRY TO RAMPS—LEADS THRO' DECONTAMINATION ROOMS TO UPPER FLOOR OF REFUGE-STATION

NOTE 1:—
REFUGE HAS THREE LEVELS: UPPER OR Nº 1 FLOOR-HOSPITALS, INWARD TRAFFIC FROM CITY : Nº 2 FLOOR-EATING AND SLEEPING QUARTERS; Nº 3 OR LOWER FLOOR RAILHEADS FOR OUTWARD BOUND REFUGEES, FOOD AND GENERAL STORAGE SPACE, ALL INTERNAL TRANSPORT (LIGHT ELECTRIC RAILCAR).

NOTE 2:—
TUNNELS TO MAIN TERMINI EQUIPPED WITH AIRLOCKS—TO PREVENT SEEPAGE OF HEAVY POISON GAS

TUNNEL TO VICTORIA

MAINLINE STATIONS—
CIVILIANS EVACUATED
FRUM REFUGE. FOOD
SUPPLIES FOR LONDON
BROUGHT HERE FOR
DISTRIBUTION.

CHARING X

J.H. OUGHTON. 38.

SAND, PEBBLES AND CLAY.

139

A barrage balloon in Hyde Park, 1943

Caption on reverse – 'In 1938 the British Balloon Command was established to protect cities and key targets such as industrial areas, ports and harbours. Balloons were intended to defend against dive bombers flying at heights up to 5,000 feet [1,500m], forcing them to fly higher and into the range of concentrated anti-aircraft fire—anti-aircraft guns could not traverse fast enough to attack aircraft flying at low altitude and high speed. By the middle of 1940 there were 1,400 balloons, a third of them over the London area'.

A baby with his personal gas mask, 1939

Caption on reverse – 'Rock-a-by-baby with gas mask. A baby's gas helmet, one of those made especially for children under two, is slung in its container from the perambulator, as a nurse tends to her knitting while airing her charge in Hyde Park'.

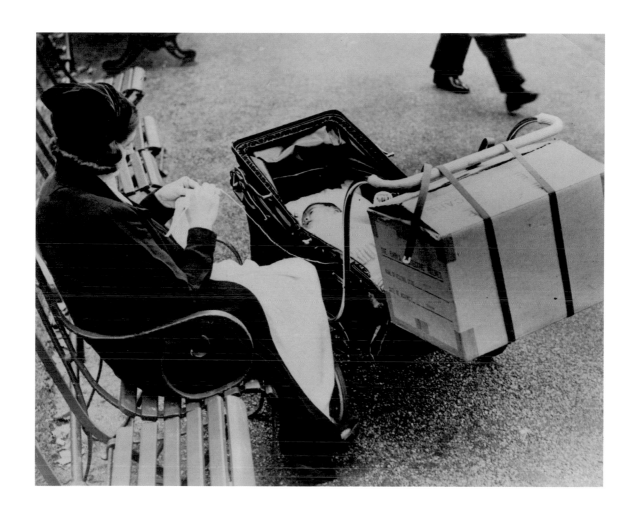

Air raid trenches in Green Park, 1940

Caption on reverse – 'Autumn 1939 finds Hyde Park apparently
deserted save for these three soldiers trudging over a blanket of
crimson-tinged leaves. Another grim note is the sign pointing the
way to the air raid trenches'.

Fire Brigade practice, Hyde Park, 1941

Caption on reverse – 'London's fire fighters keep in trim. One would imagine that when things are quiet the overworked fire fighters of London would take rest. Instead they practise to improve their flame-battling technique. This demonstration was staged in Hyde Park for the benefit of the Lord Privy Seal'.

Hyde Park as a salvage depot, 1941

Caption on reverse – 'Any kindling today? Wood and other property salvaged from bomb-blitzed sections of London are neatly piled up in the bomb salvage dump in Hyde Park'.

The Phantom Squad on manoeuvres in Richmond Park, 1941

Caption on reverse – 'During the Second World War, Pembroke Lodge in Richmond Park became the base for a military unit, the GHQ Liaison Regiment, known as the Phantom Squad. This was a special reconnaissance unit set up to report back information, using wireless communications and mobility, to provide real-time assessment from the front line in a range of battle scenes, including D-Day and Arnhem. The Phantom Squad recruited men with various skill-sets – linguists, drivers and mechanics – and undertook rigorous training in wireless communication and cipher, often in Richmond Park'.

GHQ LIAISON REGIMENT, HOME FORCES   SEPT 1940
"PHANTOM" — DRWG OC SIGNALS.   Nov. 1941.

e forces who will deal with it more
.y.

G. F. Hopkinson   Lt. Col.
                    Commanding,
s.   G.H.Q. Liaison Regiment.

→ Brigadier Comd 1st Airborne Bde
→ General " 1st " Div (N.Africa)
— Killed in Sicily on recce round Mt Etna

HQ. IN RICHMOND PARK, SURREY.

151

A model for the Peter Pan statue returns to see how he has grown, 1941

Caption on reverse – 'Peter Pan now a Lance-Corporal. James William Shaw, 41 years old Lance-Corporal who operated a searchlight in an anti-aircraft division of the British Army, strikes an attitude as he stands beside Sir George Frampton's statue of Peter Pan in Kensington Gardens. Shaw posed for the statuette of Peter Pan when he was 10 years old'.

Now that the railings are gone, 1942

Caption on reverse – 'London girls enjoy their lunch hour sunning themselves on the grass by the lake in St James's. Now that the railings which kept visitors off the grass have been removed to make munitions, thousands are daily enjoying themselves along the shores of the lake'.

An unusual sight in the Serpentine, 1943

Caption on reverse – 'US Army in England. A party of American soldiers, wearing battle kit, swim across the Serpentine during a recent demonstration'.

The aftermath of war in St James's Park, 1946

Even after the cessation of hostilities there were still dangerous issues to be resolved and rather a lot of repair work, but thankfully no one was hurt.

THE BOMB THAT TICKED IN ST. JAMES'S PARK.

THE BIG BANG: THE GERMAN 1000-LB. BOMB, WHICH HAD LAIN DORMANT IN ST. JAMES'S PARK FOR FIVE YEARS AND BEGAN TO TICK AFTER ROYAL ENGINEERS HAD DUG DOWN TO IT, EXPLODING UNDER CONTROLLED DETONATION.

BEFORE THE BANG: SAPPERS LISTENING BY EARPHONE TO THE BOMB TICKING. THE HEAD OF THE SHAFT CAN BE SEEN CENTRE-BACK.

THE CRITICAL MOMENT: DEPRESSING THE PLUNGERS TO FIRE THE GUNCOTTON CHARGES WHICH DEMOLISHED THE BOMB.

AFTER THE BANG: THE CRATER LEFT BY THE EXPLOSION OF THE 1000-LB. BOMB, 25 FT. DEEP, 40 FT. ACROSS, LITTERED WITH TIMBERS FROM THE SHAFT.

AT 7.12 p.m. on April 26 the German 1000-lb. "ticking" bomb which had lain dormant under a footpath in St. James's Park since April 1941, was exploded by a Royal Engineers Bomb Disposal squad. Two days previously, as some of the men were working in the shaft, the bomb began to tick. As this meant that the bomb might explode at any moment, work was discontinued in the shaft, the park was closed to the public and warnings were sent to Buckingham Palace and Marlborough House. For two days intermittent ticking could be heard by the bomb-detecting apparatus, but at 7 p.m. on April 26 "zero hour" was reached without incident and the bomb was demolished with two 4-lb. guncotton charges. At the time of the explosion (which was broadcast by the B.B.C.) Princess Elizabeth was at Buckingham Palace and Queen Mary in residence at Marlborough House. Less than a quarter of an hour after the explosion Queen Mary came out and inspected the crater.

'Over the centuries of their shared heritage, the parks have steadily evolved from private royal hunting grounds to much loved public parks.'

4   PEOPLE AT PLAY

Over the centuries of their shared heritage, the Parks have steadily evolved from private royal hunting grounds to much loved public parks. Their wide spaces, ease of access and attractive scenery have made them focal points for a diverse range of sporting activities as well as facilitating a vast array of recreational pursuits for all to enjoy.

In London, the transition from royal hunting grounds to public parks began slowly, with promenading as the first public leisure activity in the Parks. The central London parks became the place to be seen, with the aristocracy displaying their elaborate attire as they promenaded along Queen's Walk in St James's Park or paraded with fine horses and carriages in the Ring in Hyde Park. Where once one might have seen only the King and Prime Minister chasing a stag, as George II and Sir Robert Walpole were inclined to do, today one can see roller-bladers, roller-skiers, boaters, open-water swimmers, tennis players, joggers and cyclists, from all walks of life.

In winter, the frozen lakes offered a different experience, as the public flocked to the Parks to skate. This popularity proved tragic in 1867 when the ice buckled, resulting in 40 deaths. Green Park and Richmond Park were home to early ballooning attempts in the late 1780s. Hyde Park and Primrose Hill were sites of 18th-century duels and prize fights. Pall Mall and the Mall derive their names from the game of 'paille-maille' (an old French game resembling croquet) enjoyed by Charles II in St James's Park.

Team sports have been an enduring feature in all the Parks. Today the Hub in Regent's Park is the largest outdoor sports area in Central London, and cricket, football and rugby are played in other parks. Richmond Park is home to two 18-hole public golf courses and has just hosted its first polo match for 150 years.

Some of the oldest and most successful sports clubs have been formed and nurtured in the Phoenix Park. These included cricket, golf (a golf course was created in 1885 and existed for a few years) and motor sport in particular. In the latter half of the 19th century the Park became more intensively used for football, hurling, cricket and other sports. Tradition has it that in 1879 a meeting between Michael Cusack and Pat Nally held in Phoenix Park was one of the first steps in founding the Gaelic Athletic Association (GAA).

The Zoological Gardens, common to both Regent's Park and Phoenix Park, are famous and popular features, each attracting well over a million visitors a year. Decimus Burton, the architect of London Zoo, which opened for study in 1828 and to the public in 1847, was invited to design a zoo for Dublin. In 1840, with 46 mammals and 72 birds donated by London Zoo, Dublin Zoo opened to the public on Sundays, 'admission one penny'.

Phoenix Park is increasingly used by the public for a range of recreational activities. In the beginning of the 20th century, motor racing speed trials were a major attraction, along with international motor racing, which commenced in 1929. More recent celebrations and entertainments which attract large numbers have been associated with the papal visit, band concerts, sporting events, charity runs and Bloom, the highly successful garden and food show.

St James's Park was the favourite site of comedies and evening entertainment for high society in the 18th century, with facetious pieces such as 'Love in a Wood, or St James's Park' set here. Now Regent's Park hosts an open-air theatre while Hyde Park has become the setting for the ever popular Winter Wonderland festival.

Music in the London Parks began with small concerts in bandstands and has grown steadily into large concerts in Hyde Park and global benefit concerts like Live 8 in 2005. The Parks are also intimately connected with film, as the world's first moving picture was filmed near Apsley Gate in Hyde Park in 1889. Since then Genevieve (1953), Johnny English (2003) and Stormbreaker (2006) all have scenes filmed in Hyde Park, while Richmond Park stars in Anne of a Thousand Days (1969).

Now, for many visitors the Parks are oases of tranquillity in which to observe nature, enjoy sport, walk, jog, run, cycle or exercise their pets and long may they remain so.

'About 87 million people use the Royal Parks and Phoenix Park annually.'

George Morland (after Soiron; engraved by Thomas Gaugain), *St James's Park,* **1790**

St James's Park in the 18th century was still partially rural, where milkwomen grazed their cows. They earned their living by selling absolutely fresh milk at one penny per mug. Trade developed sufficiently to justify construction of the 'lactarian', a kiosk for milk sales which remained in the park until about a century ago.

St. James's Park.

Maria Spilsbury (engraved by James Godby), *The Drinking Well in Hyde Park,* 1802

This painting depicts a rural scene, perhaps with some artistic licence. The Drinking Well was located in 'The Ring', a very popular and fashionable enclosure for promenading and refreshments, especially on Sundays.

Although drinking water is now supplied as mains water from fountains, spring water is still used extensively for irrigation.

Crinoline in Dublin, Phoenix Park, colour print by McCleary Wightman, mid-19th century

The celebrated diarist Mrs Delany, on her first visit to Dublin in 1731, wrote, 'As a fashionable place of recreation, the Park enjoyed great renown. It far exceeded in beauty the London parks. Its large extent, its fine turf and its agreeable prospects are mentioned and to crown all a ring in the midst of a delightful wood, intersected with glades, was the resort of beaux and belles in fair weather'.

The Park was a popular place for driving, a term we now might call sightseeing or touring. In 1836 the Dublin Penny Journal recorded that 'of the various pleasant drives round the city, that through the Park by the side of the Liffey appears to be the most esteemed by the citizens.

A drive on a box seat of a well-appointed four-in-hand on a fine day was most enjoyable and invigorating. Although there are carriages and coaches of all descriptions, the jaunting car is the national vehicle – charge 8d. [pence] and in some cases 6d. a mile. The charge for a carriage is sixteen or eighteen pence'.

CRINOLINE IN DUBLIN
PHŒNIX PARK

William F. Witherington, *The Earl of Dysart's Family in Richmond Park,* mid-19th century

Picnics were a popular Victorian leisure activity and this oil painting captures the Dysart family, of nearby Ham House, enjoying this pastime in the park. The location is on high ground looking over what is now a public golf course and Beverly Brook to the spire of St Matthias church.

This lovely painting was purchased by telephone bidding to an auction house in New Hampshire, USA. When the auctioneer's hammer fell, the clerk exclaimed in a voice reminiscent of the film character ET, 'Folks, it's going home to Richmond Park, it's going home', to enthusiastic applause.

Henry Barraud (engraved by WH Simmons), *Rotten Row, Hyde Park,* **1864**

This unusually large print shows the popularity of Rotten Row for promenading on foot and by carriage.

The foreground has detailed depictions of high society Londoners in their finery as well as Alexandra, then Princess of Wales, followed by Edward, Prince of Wales, Prince Alfred and Prince George, Duke of Cambridge. Careful examination reveals some odd pets.

The background shows part of Apsley House, the screen by Decimus Burton, the Wellington Arch with the statue still in place and St George's hospital, now the Lanesborough Hotel.

John Hardman Powell (1827-1895), *Cricket in Phoenix Park, Dublin*

This tranquil scene in Phoenix Park depicts a long tradition of cricket within the Park. The earliest match in Ireland whose details survive was played on the Fifteen Acres in Phoenix Park in August 1792 between an eleven of the Garrison and an All Ireland side. One of the players was the future Duke of Wellington, then aged 23, who was noted in the match report to have been a promising player.

The first club to establish their home in the Phoenix Park was the Phoenix Cricket Club when they were allocated a 150-square yard area by the Commissioners of Woods and Forests in 1838 between the Wellington Testimonial and Chesterfield Road. The Phoenix Club was founded around 1830 and is the oldest club in Ireland.

The Civil Service Cricket Club was formed in Phoenix Park in 1863 with the assistance of the Lord Lieutenant, the Earl of Carlisle, who was a cricket enthusiast. The Club played their first match in the grounds of Áras an Uachtaráin (then the Viceregal demesne) in 1863. Their grounds are located between the Wellington Testimonial and the Citadel or Dog pond. Both clubs still thrive in Phoenix Park.

The Zoological Gardens (Dublin Zoo), Phoenix Park, Dublin, late 19th century

The original gatehouse entrance to Dublin Zoo still survives, though somewhat altered, but with its original front steps and railings. In May 1830, at a meeting in the Rotunda in Dublin, it was decided to establish the Zoological Society of Dublin with the aim of forming a living collection of animals, similar to London Zoo in Regent's Park which had opened to the public in 1828.

The Zoological Society appointed Decimus Burton (then architect to London Zoo) to draw up a report and plans for the picturesque three-acre Phoenix Park site. This area was gradually expanded over the decades to its present area of around 60 acres, half of which was transferred from the Áras demesne in the 1990s.

Its present size has allowed a much more ecological approach to be adopted for animal welfare, with appropriate planting and the provision of larger animal habitats. A very successful breeding and educational programme is in place and Dublin Zoo is now a major visitor attraction.

ZOOLOGICAL GARDENS. DUBLIN. 2176. W. L.

177

Feeding the peacocks in Kensington Gardens, 1891

Ornamental birds and animals have a long history in the parks. King James I had a veritable menagerie in St James's Park, including hawks, antelopes, crocodiles, a leopard and an 'ellefant', whose diet including a gallon of wine a day. In Victorian times the emphasis was on public spectacle rather than animal welfare.

The Royal Parks have responded well to society's changing views by focusing on the conservation of native species in natural habitats, with designated sanctuaries and dedicated wildlife officers. This work across all the parks is exemplified by the international recognition of Richmond Park as a Special Area of Conservation.

FEEDING THE PEACOCKS IN KENSINGTON GARDENS

DRAWN BY PERCY MACQUOID, R.I.

The first motor-car in Hyde Park, 1897

The use of cars in the parks began in a small-scale way, now quaint to our eyes, over a century ago. In the early years, popular time trials and races were held. As car use expanded exponentially so did the impact on the parks. More roads were created and surfaced with tarmac, while some visitors began to notice the disadvantages of the noise.

Although cars give people mobility and access to enjoy the open spaces, it is challenging to find a way of maintaining these benefits as well as the tranquillity of the parks.

THE FIRST MOTOR-CAR IN HYDE PARK.

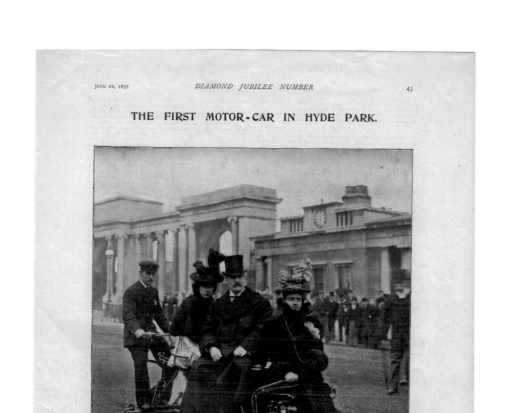

THE PENNINGTON MOTOR-CAR

The Walter Sexton Memorial Trophy (silver) and Presentation Book

Walter Sexton, the Honorary Secretary of the Royal Irish Automobile Club, was responsible for most of the organisation of the Irish Grand Prix. This comprised three international motor races which were staged in Phoenix Park in three consecutive years, commencing in 1929. The races were a huge success and Sexton's colleagues presented him with a replica silver Phoenix Trophy, along with a signed presentation book.

The Walter Sexton Trophy was first awarded in 1949 and since then it has become the most highly prized in Irish motor sport, with the names of some of the greatest drivers gracing it.

Phoenix Park was also the location for the 1903 motor speed trials element of the Gordon Bennett Race. These were held over a two-week period throughout the country in July of that year. At the Phoenix Park speed trials Baron de Forest set a new world record time for the flying kilometre of 85.9 mph.

A polo match in Phoenix Park, August 1896

In August 1874 the All Ireland Polo Club (AIPC) was granted permission to erect a tent in Phoenix Park for four days during the Horse Show that year, which was held in the Royal Dublin Society's showgrounds at Ballsbridge in Dublin.

The polo ground is located on the Nine Acres, near Dublin Zoo. This ground is now recognised as the oldest polo ground in Europe in continuous use. Sadly, the first recorded polo fatality occurred in Phoenix Park in 1877, when Robert Darley was fatally injured when his pony tripped and fell. At the time no player wore protective headgear.

Another form of polo is cycle polo which is also played in Phoenix Park and in a small number of areas throughout the country. The game was invented in County Wicklow, Ireland, in 1891 by Richard J. Mecredy, who was a retired champion cyclist at the time. The first game of cycle polo was played at the Scalp, County Wicklow in the same year. An international cycle polo match was played in Phoenix Park in 1937 on the army grounds.

Polo matches attracted large numbers of spectators who enjoyed free admission, because grounds in the Phoenix Park could not be allocated exclusively to any particular group.

Boy Scouts camping, 1914

Caption on reverse – 'Boys camp in Hyde Park. Five boys of the
9th Westminster troop of Boy Scouts are spending their holidays
camping in Hyde Park. They have a complete outfit and cook all their
own meals'.

Just a century ago, the young clearly enjoyed self-sufficiency and
engaging with nature.

Rowing in Regent's Park, 1922

Caption on reverse – 'Blind oarsmen practising at Regent's Park for St Dunstan's Regatta which is to be held at Putney tomorrow (Tuesday)'.

Wonderful proof that parks can and do provide recreation for all.

Learning to ride in Richmond Park, 1933

In this photograph we see a uniformed Lyons Teashop waitress (known as a 'Nippy') riding a horse. Although the horse is not being helpful, the rider still appears to be enjoying herself.

The Serpentine Lido, Hyde Park, 1933

Caption on reverse – 'At London's 'Coney Island', seeking relief from London's sweltering heat early in August, crowds at the Hyde Park Lido, in the British metropolis, in as little as the law allows'.

The Lido was opened in 1930 at the initiative of George Lansbury, the first Commissioner of Works. It was a great success, attracting up to 95,000 annual visitors and is still used today.

The Pearly King and Queen with winning donkey, Pretty Polly, in Regent's Park, 1943

Caption on reverse – 'Bert Matthews and his queen, the King and Queen of Hampstead costers, giving their donkey Pretty Polly a cooling drink from the Queen Alexandra Cup which it won as the best donkey at the Street Traders and Costers Show in Regent's Park'.

A costermonger is a street seller of fruit and vegetables and the Pearlies, founded in 1911, wearing clothes decorated with mother-of-pearl buttons, continue to raise funds for London-based charities.

Winner of all-clothes swimming race in the Serpentine, 1938

Caption on reverse – 'Youth winner in All-Clothes Race in Serpentine, London. Thomas, 16- year-old winner of the 100 yards is carried from the stream on the soaked shoulders of the other competitors for the Mrs Kerr Smiley Trophy. It was the first time that the youth had competed in this type of swimming race'.

197

An Irish Guard and a British woman exchange glances, 1948

Caption on reverse – 'Old Look and New Look in Hyde Park. A member of the Irish Guards and a British woman exchange glances while strolling in opposite directions in London's Hyde Park. The kilt he's wearing made its first appearance in 1666. She wears a plaid skirt with the new, long hemline'.

An amusing photograph that epitomises the warmth of Anglo-Irish relations.

Lunchtime in St James's Park, 1952

Caption on reverse – 'Slow Pace – Lunch Time'.

Total relaxation is one of the most important benefits of these
tranquil parks.

At the Round Pond – Mr John Farr with his model fishing boat, 1967

Caption on reverse – 'Scene at the Round Pond in Kensington Gardens yesterday – which is a miniature sea with miniature waves beating against miniature shores. It also has miniature boats, built with such a respect for accuracy that you half expect the miniature crew to emerge from the hatches'.

Kensington Palace is the grand background to this charming scene by the Round Pond of young and old enjoying Kensington Gardens.

The iconic Rolling Stones concert, Hyde Park, 1969

Caption on reverse – 'Some of the 250,000 fans of the pop group Rolling Stones dance enthusiastically during a free concert in a corner of Hyde park here July 5th. The concert, the first by the Stones in 14 months and which had been planned months before, turned into a requiem of pure rock for former Stone's guitarist Brian Jones, who was drowned in the swimming pool of his London home, July 3rd'.

Although some disapprove of these concerts, it is undeniable that many people enjoy them and that they create much needed income for the parks.

Walking the leopard, 1970

Caption on reverse – 'Secretary Angela McWilliams takes Michael, her pet leopard, down to Kensington Gardens for his daily walk. He came from the Tyseley Pet Stores in Birmingham, at a price of £200. The cat lives with Angela in her Kensington flat'.

Perhaps the strangest pet to be exercised in Kensington Gardens?

Speakers' Corner, Hyde Park, 1971

Caption on reverse – 'Speakers' Corner is a traditional site for public speeches and debates since the mid-1800s, when protests and demonstrations took place in Hyde Park.

Historic figures such as Karl Marx, Vladimir Lenin and George Orwell were known to often use the area to demonstrate free speech.

In 1872, an Act of Parliament set aside this part of Hyde Park for public speaking. Even today, on a Sunday morning, it's not unusual to find crowds gathering at Speakers' Corner to listen to enthusiasts expounding their views. Anyone can turn up unannounced to speak on any subject, as long as the police consider their speeches lawful'.

Sailing on the Serpentine, 1980

Caption on reverse – 'January 10th 1980. Top yachtsmen [Patterson and Musto] sail the Serpentine in aid of British Olympic yachting and the Fastnet disaster.

Rodney Patterson, Britain's triple Olympic medallist, today completed a series of races by six-men teams, representing Olympic yachting and the Royal Ocean Racing Club, on the Serpentine in aid of British Olympic yachting and the Fastnet disaster. Rodney was among crewmen rescued during the race in August 1979'.

Athletics in Phoenix Park, 2011

The runners in this photograph are participants in the Dublin Half Marathon on 17 September 2011. This race is one of a large number of road races, cross country, triathlons, duathlons and cycle races – some of which are charity events – that take place in Phoenix Park annually.

Before the formation of the Gaelic Athletic Association (GAA) in 1884, athletics appears to have been limited to universities, the garrison and the 'elite'. In 1924, the Irish Government supported the revival of an ancient sporting festival known as the Táilteann Games (called after Queen Táilte). Two segments of the sporting festival were held in Phoenix Park – the swimming competition, in which the famous Johnny Weissmuller (star of the Tarzan films) competed in the pond at Dublin Zoo, and the most popular event, the motor racing, which drew thousands of spectators.

Other notable sporting events, both of which were held on Chesterfield Road, included Bob Geldof's 'Live Aid' run in 1986 and the finish of the first stage of the Tour de France in 1997, when it was held for the first time in Ireland.

'Our ancestors have left us a
wonderful legacy; let us honour it.'

5 PARK MANAGEMENT

The management of Phoenix Park almost since its formation in 1662 was entrusted to a Ranger and his department; this was also the case with the English Royal Parks. Important functions such as security and protection of game rested with the Ranger's department. The early Rangers of the London Parks were individuals of high status: Richmond Park was entrusted to Lord Walpole, before being passed to Princess Amelia and then to George III. Bushy Park was held by the wife of Lord North, the Prime Minister, before being passed to the future William IV. Hyde Park and St James's Park were once entrusted to the great Anglo-Irish soldier and statesman, Arthur Wellesley, first Duke of Wellington.

In Phoenix Park, routine maintenance and building works were undertaken in the 17th century by the Royal Works and then by the Surveyor General's Department and Barrack Board in the 18th century, which later became the Irish Board of Works and the Barrack Board.

With the appointment of Decimus Burton major landscape and architectural works took place between 1832 and 1849 in Phoenix Park. Burton's reputation had already been well established with Woods & Forests through his works on the Royal Parks in London, including his designs for lodges and gateways in Hyde Park which he provided in 1825.

Burton was also influential in changing management practices by introducing byelaws from the Royal Parks in London as well as a dress code for the Park Constables and Gate Keepers. He also insisted on replacing the female gatekeepers (who also hung out their washing at the gates) with male operatives.

At first glance the Parks may appear natural and in need of little management. This would have been partly correct in the early days, when the deer were the simple priority. Leg of Mutton and other ponds in Richmond Park were dug by hand to provide drinking water. In winter the deer were fed daily because grass contains insufficient nutrients. This feeding still continues, but delivered by Land Rover rather than by horse and cart. Deer keepers were entrusted with the care of the herds and on occasion fought pitched gun battles with deer stealers.

Some unusual work was prompted by the death of William III in 1702. The King died as a result of complications of a fall thought to have been caused by his horse Sorrel tripping on a molehill in Richmond Park. Thus a mole-catcher's cottage was built and subsequently much enlarged to become Pembroke Lodge.

Many attempts were made to introduce new game to the London Parks, from turkeys in Richmond Park by George II to pheasants in St James's Park, though few have endured. Ornamental birds fared best, as shown by the pelicans in St James's Park introduced in 1664 by the Russian ambassador.

As large unlit areas, the Parks attracted crime, with highwaymen camping in Green Park. Thus the 'Route du

Roi' (or Rotten Row) in Hyde Park was lit with 300 oil lamps, the first artificially lit highway. In 1872 the Royal Parks' Keepers were established and, unusually for the time, given all the powers of police constables. The Royal Parks unit of the Metropolitan Police remains, but is much reduced.

Increased public access required provision and management of a much wider range of facilities, including security, roads, paths, car parks, sporting venues, concert venues, refreshments and conveniences.

Our ancestors have left us a wonderful legacy; let us honour it and remember the words of Timothy Bennett in 1754, a shoemaker from Hampton who campaigned for public access to Bushy Park: 'I am unwilling to leave the world a worse place than I found it'.

This exhibition is a significant way of highlighting the impressive shared heritage of these unique parks and the importance of working together to preserve them for future generations.

'This exhibition is a significant way of highlighting the impressive shared heritage of these unique parks and the importance of working together to preserve them for future generations.'

William Spalding Wilkie, Park bailiff 1832-1870

William Spalding Wilkie served as head gardener to Under-secretaries Gregory and Gosset at the Under-secretary's demesne (now the Phoenix Park Visitor Centre) for about sixteen years, before his appointments as under-bailiff and bailiff.

He came highly recommended from Woburn Abbey, home of the Dukes of Bedford, where he had assisted in the production of *Hortus gramineus woburnensis* (1824), a descriptive catalogue which contained numerous specimens of dried grasses.

When he died at his White Fields residence in Phoenix Park in February 1870, at the age of 76, Wilkie had served as under-bailiff and bailiff for 38 years, thus spanning the entire management period of the Park under Woods and Forests, the Board of Works (GB) and ten years of management under the Board of Works (Irl) from 1860 to 1870.

Wilkie was a man of great managerial ability and had a well-developed artistic talent in landscape design.

219

An outbreak of rabies, 1888

Like any deer, the deer herds in Dublin and London are susceptible to many diseases, some of which could destroy entire herds. The 1888 rabies outbreak had become established but was stopped by firm rapid action, which was also necessary in the 21st century to protect the deer from foot-and-mouth disease.

As international trade, travel and park visitor numbers increase so does the range of threats. Dutch elm disease caused widespread damage and more pests and diseases now threaten trees. The control of just one pest, the oak processionary moth, diverts resources from other essential work.

REPORTS

ON THE

OUTBREAK OF RABIES

AMONG

DEER

IN

RICHMOND PARK DURING THE YEARS 1886-7,

BY

Mr. A. C. COPE,

CHIEF INSPECTOR, AGRICULTURAL DEPARTMENT, PRIVY COUNCIL OFFICE,

AND

Professor VICTOR HORSLEY, B.S., F.R.S., &c.,

PROF. SUPERINTENDENT OF THE BROWN INSTITUTION, WANDSWORTH ROAD, S.W.

Presented to both Houses of Parliament by Command of Her Majesty.

LONDON:
PRINTED FOR HER MAJESTY'S STATIONERY OFFICE,
BY EYRE AND SPOTTISWOODE,
PRINTERS TO THE QUEEN'S MOST EXCELLENT MAJESTY.

And to be purchased, either directly or through any Bookseller, from
EYRE AND SPOTTISWOODE, EAST HARDING STREET, FLEET STREET, E.C.; and
32, Abingdon Street, Westminster, S.W.; or
ADAM AND CHARLES BLACK, 6, NORTH BRIDGE, EDINBURGH; or
HODGES, FIGGIS & Co., 104, GRAFTON STREET, DUBLIN.

1888.

[C.—5276.]

Books of Regulations and Accounts

a) Deer Account (book) from 24th November 1905 to 24th November 1950.
b) Phoenix Park. Regulations To Be Observed By the Deer-keeper, Gate Keepers and Constables of His Majesty's Phoenix Park, Dublin (1902)
c) Páirc an Fhionn-Uisce (Phoenix Park). Regulations to be observed by the Deer-keeper, Gate-keepers and Constables of the Phoenix Park, Dublin (1926)
d) Saorstát Éireann. Statutory Rules and Orders (1926), No.6, Phoenix Park, Dublin, Byelaws (1926)

These books contain the regulations and byelaws which govern the management of Phoenix Park. They were issued to the deer keeper, gate keepers and constables to enable them to undertake their duties.

The head deer keeper, who was in charge of the Park constables and gate keepers, had the general care of the Park under his remit as well as the responsibilty for ensuring that the Park constables and gate keepers attended to their duties in their respective districts and at designated gates.

However, his primary responsibility was to take care of the deer and cattle grazing and to furnish the bailiff with a deer count taken on 24 November each year. Up until 1841 this had not taken place. Why this particular date was chosen annually is unclear but possibly, with the foliage gone from the trees and the undergrowth dying back, visibility would have been clearer.

Each morning the head deer keeper and Park constables attended the bailiff's lodge and reported any wrong doing that might have occurred since the previous morning as well as receiving new instructions from the Park bailiff.

The Dogs' Acre in Hyde Park, 1899

This cemetery for beloved pets is typical of the kind public spirit of those who work in the parks of London and Dublin.

In 1881 the gatekeeper at Victoria Lodge, Mr Winbridge, and his superiors agreed to allow a grave in his garden for the dog of grieving owners Mr and Mrs Lewis Barned, who were regular park visitors. Their beloved Maltese terrier Cherry was laid to rest with the memorial: Poor Cherry. Died April 28, 1881.

News of this kindness spread rapidly and by 1903 the garden was filled with over 300 graves and no more could be accepted. But, as ever, every effort was made to help park visitors, even with unusual requests.

THE DOG'S ACRE IN HYDE PARK.

From Photographs by Boias, Oxford Street, W.

No one who rambles omnibusly westward from the Marble Arch along Bayswater Road, rattles in a hansom, or walks sedately, if not in state, past Victoria Gate, can fail to notice on his left hand, behind the railings of the Park and under the shadow of the great houses on the other side of the way, the rows of little white tombstones which make the Dogs' Cemetery a distinctive, and in many respects a distinguished spot. Here the remains of many a four-footed friend of sentimental woman and tender-hearted man sleep the long sleep, unforgotten in death as beloved in life, as many tributes testify. Prosaic, indeed, was its beginning, for it is in reality merely the little garden attached to the lodge of the gate keeper, who inaugurated the cemetery and made the little plot of ground a veritable Garden of Sleep, and who has only recently himself laid down his work, folded his hands, and closed his eyes on the labour of this world. Not without a touch of sentiment has been its continuation, soon to reach a point of sorrow, when it is closed, as it must inevitably be before very long.

The rectilineal plot, cut into at one end by the semicircular wall belonging to the lodge, is appropriately planted, by chance— or was it design?—with ivy and laurel, symbol of immortality, with bushes of dark-green myrtle, classic symbol of death, and here and there with a bright-berried holly-tree, whose red gleams hopefully and suggestively out of the green. Beautifully kept, its tiny pathways lined with brown tiles, the little graves arranged in rows, overgrown with green bushes and flowering plants, this Garden of Death, like so many within the City's walls, is full almost to overflowing, and, in the nature of things, can become the abiding-place of but a few more inhabitants whose epitaphs will bear witness to their worth. Unlike mere men, however, the evil they may perchance have done is interred with them, and only the good lives after them. The Bible has been freely drawn upon by these devoted friends of the dog. On the tomb of more than one of these departed creatures may be read the words from Luke xii. 6—

Not one of them is forgotten before God.

Now and again one comes across the grave of a cat, as, for example—

In memoriam, Chinchilla (Chilla), Lovely, loving, and most dearly loved. Poisoned July 31st, 1895. God restore thee to me, so prayeth thy ever-loving mistress Elene;

the last word being in Greek characters, while beneath are many Egyptian hieroglyphs Another stone, with fuller details still, is a tribute to—

My faithful Minnie, Yorkshire terrier. Weight, 3½ lb. Died February 27th, 1896; and beautiful Pat, died July 29th, 1895. Ever remembered. Friends to Bobby over the way "They were lovely and pleasant in their lives, And in their death they were not divided."

On another tombstone is the inscription—

Alas, poor Zoo! Born 1st of October, 1878; died 13th of August, 1892. As deeply mourned as ever dog was mourned, For friendship rare by her adorned.

One stone is raised to the memory of "Darling Doley, my sunbeam, my consolation, my joy," whose life-race was run from 1882 to 1898. "Pilku, au revoir," is the simple inscription engraved upon another stone. Not good-bye, note, but "au revoir"; and over the words is the device of a serpent around a cross, placed in an inverted crown, and beneath a dove with expanded wings, symbol of immortality. Close by, another white stone raises its head to "Jack the Dandy, a sportsman and a pal," whose name a wreath of now discoloured ivy, its red berries standing out in vivid contrast, attests is still held in tender memory. Is there not a wealth of pathos in this epitaph to "Curly, a faithful friend, who pined for his lost mistress, and died 19th November, 1896"?

Almost every little stone carries some individuality of its own, and, therefore, conspicuous by reason of its very plainness and simplicity in the serried rows of white marble is a short, thick, green board, painted, with discoloured white letters, "In memory of Fly," and with a date now no longer to be deciphered, as the inscription is bespattered with mud. Equally conspicuous is another at one of the far corners, in the prosaic shadow of the gardener's tool-house, near an out-of-place litter of bottles, jam-pots, and jars. It is covered with a pile of decayed wreaths, of which there must be at least fifty or sixty, to bear witness to a long period of mourning, for, as the inquirer may learn, one was sent regularly every week. So the list might be extended from the earliest interment to the last two, which are but a few days old. The graves are still unplanted with flowers or evergreen, and on them still lie withering the bunches of violets which kindly hands have placed there, sweet tributes to dead love. These two graves lie close together, and tell of "Max, died February 19th, 1899," a loving, faithful friend," and of "Darling Jockie, a loving friend and companion; died February 18th, 1899."

Nor are fresh flowers absent from these tiny tombs. Violets wither, tulips pale, lilies give all their sweetness over the mortal remains of these departed dogs. Growing plants cover a tombstone which bears the inscription, "A mon cher Wee. Mes Pensées. 23rd Avril, 1895," and in vases may be seen bunches of violets and primroses which have evidently only just been placed there, and are constantly renewed; while a little further on a stone has been erected "To dear little Ami. Unvergesslich. Died 24th February, 1898," which has been decked on the anniversary with a wreath of white lilies and bright-green leaves and ferns.

There is, indeed, little to differentiate in sentiment this burial-place from that in which loving hands consign the remains of loved human bodies. Nor is the interment, as a rule, a careless or a callous one. The body of the pet, laid in a box, is taken to the lodge, with, not seldom, an undertaker, to add dignity to a ceremony not without its touch of distinction. Following the remains may sometimes be seen a human friend, dressed in black, or else a representative, to see that the last rites are paid properly and soberly rendered to a mite which once brought not a little joy into an otherwise companionless and empty life.

Jack's headstone, in the grounds of Áras an Uachtaráin (formerly the Viceregal Demesne)

When King Edward VII visited the Viceregal Lodge in 1903, he was accompanied by his dog Jack. Sadly, shortly after his arrival, the dog was found dead in the grounds. The German staff surgeon cried out 'Der Hund ist tot' (the dog is dead). Jack was buried beside one of the quiet walks in the demesne and a simple inscribed tablet placed over the grave.

The Viceroy at the time was Lord Dudley and to make amends for the loss he said he would replace the dog. The replacement was a wire-haired fox terrier named Caesar. On its arrival, the dog was locked in a room where the Field Marshal's uniform lay in which the King was meant to review the troops in Phoenix Park the next day. It was found, however, that Caesar had chewed the Field Marshal's boots. The King laughed and reviewed the army in the uniform of the Admiral of the Fleet instead.

Notwithstanding his mischievous start, Caesar quickly became a great pet and accompanied his master abroad. On his collar was a tag inscribed 'I am Caesar, the King's dog'.

At King Edward's funeral in 1910, the King's charger and Caesar were led immediately behind the coffin.

HERE:LIES
"JACK"
KING:EDWARD'S
FAVOVRITE:IRISH:TERRIER

WHO:ONLY:LIVED:TWELVE:HOVRS
AFTER:REACHING:HIS:NATIVE:LAND
HE:DIED:AT:THE:VICEREGAL:LODGE
ON
JVLY:21:1903

Police control Fascist rally in Hyde Park, 1934

Caption on reverse – 'Police are shown struggling to hold back the great crowd as Sir Oswald Mosley, leader of the British Union of Fascists, arrived in Hyde Park to address the rally of Blackshirts. Several persons were injured when the fascists clashed with Reds and other anti-fascists'.

Our tradition of free speech at Speakers' Corner, the centrality of Hyde Park and its large open spaces have attracted demonstrations for every imaginable cause for over 200 years. Most are peaceful but still require management. Between 1855 and 1866 there were many large violent demonstrations of up to 150,000 people, causing loss of life, many injuries and much damage to the park.

On 1 April 1867 the Royal Parks Constabulary took responsibility for policing, subsequently transferred to the Metropolitan Police. Although the officers in the separate command unit are dedicated, their numbers have been halved while visitor numbers have doubled.

Parkgate Street Police Barracks, c.1930

This photograph records the handing over of the Dublin Metropolitan Police Barracks at the Park's main entrance to Jack (John) Manning (gatekeeper), who received it on behalf of the Office of Public Works. Manning was stationed at this location at the time and resided in the gatelodge opposite.

The Dublin Metropolitan Police were formed in 1786 and performed a vital role in Park security, especially from 1837 onwards. The DMP, as they were known, had the overall responsibility for policing Dublin city, were unarmed, and came under the control of a commissioner of police whose administrative headquarters was at Dublin Castle. Another police barracks was built (1848) in the Park at Ashtown Gate and was warmly welcomed by the twenty-seven-strong police force (required to protect the Park) especially after the winter of 1847, which was one of the severest on record.

Peelers and Bobbies are names by which the police are sometimes, even yet, referred to. They were embodied under an Act brought in by Sir Robert Peel about 1820. In 1823 it was extended to all Ireland. Sir Robert Peel served as Chief Secretary for Ireland from 1812 to 1818 and again from 1861 to 1865.

In 1839 an Act was passed to provide 'for the better training of a Reserve [police] force, to be kept at or near Dublin'. This resulted in the building of the Phoenix Park Depot which catered for between six and seven hundred men. These facilities are now used by An Garda Síochána (Irish Police Force) as their main depot and previously as their training depot.

Gas light and lighter, Phoenix Park, 1974

In the 1859 Park estimates, over £800 was included for the provision of gas lighting of Chesterfield Road from Parkgate Street to Castleknock Gate, resulting from public pressure from the residents of Castleknock and the immediate locality.

Decimus Burton added gas lights around the resited Phoenix Column as part of his realignment of the Chesterfield Road in the 1840s and gas lights were also strategically placed around the Gough Monument. These were subsequently replaced with mirror- backed gas lights which increased the illumination reflected onto the monument.

The five lamplighters required to turn on and off the lamps gathered each evening outside the Hole-in-the Wall pub at sundown. All were Flanagans and more than three generations have been attending to the gas lights in the Park.

As a result of the 1986 Phoenix Park conservation management plan, the gas lighting, which uses natural gas as its source, was upgraded by increasing the number of gas lights and fitting each of the gas lanterns with additional mantels to increase the intensity of light.

The Achilles statue is cleaned, 1934

Caption on reverse – 'Achilles loses Battle of Bath. This unusual photograph shows the statue of Achilles apparently about to hurl from his shield the daring mortal who's engaged in giving him a general clean on October 29th. But it's the angle from which the picture was taken that produces that effect – actually Achilles put up with the indignity of his public bath without protest'.

Another unexpected role of the Royal Parks is memorial maintenance. Although erected for good reason to commemorate momentous events, the maintenance and restoration of the memorials is both specialist and costly.

235

Sheep in Kensington Gardens, March 1949

Caption on reverse – 'Spring brought more than sunshine to the city. With it came a flock of sheep from Ayrshire (Scotland) to graze in Kensington Gardens, surrounded by the roar of traffic. Guarding the flock is 60-year-old George Walbran, shepherd for 45 years on the Yorkshire moors, with his two Border Collies, Tess, 3, and Dot, 8. City-bred dogs, unused to sheep, are their biggest worry'.

Just two generations ago, sheep grazed in Central London. Although the sheep have gone, the problems of uncontrolled dogs remain, with five deer killed in 2016 in Richmond Park alone.

Feeding the deer in Richmond Park, 1956

Caption on reverse – 'Twice a day, a tractor towing a trailer full of beans tours Richmond Park to feed 700 deer during the wintery weather'.

For centuries the deer have required winter feeding which continues to this day. Landrovers and specialist feed have replaced carts and hay. The feeding now takes place at night because of the volume of day visitors.

Rag week students go a little too far, Hyde Park, 1966

Caption on reverse – 'Soap foam battle in Hyde Park. Two hundred students fought a battle with soap foam in Hyde Park yesterday. It was to publicise Farnborough Technical College's Rag Week. The students, split into two forces, clashed along the Park's Serpentine Road in a battle of bubbles. The foam, squirted from soap dispensers, flew over photographers, policemen and a police car as well as other students themselves. But the law turned a tolerant blind eye until the students attacked a 30 ft statue put up in tribute to the Duke of Wellington'.

Management of the parks requires many judgement calls, from major to minor. In this case, typically, the staff accepted being 'foamed' themselves but drew a reasonable line at potential damage to the memorial to a great Anglo-Irish general and statesman.

Tree planting in Richmond Park, *c.*1970

Caption on reverse – 'Park staff planting a sapling, using a digger truck driven by Barry Day, who worked diligently in Richmond Park for over 40 years'.

Few visitors know that such long service in the parks of London and Dublin is common or that these landscapes require considerable management 'to preserve and enhance them for this and future generations'.

A demonstration with a difference, 1969

Caption on reverse – 'Among the various demonstrations and meetings held at Speakers' Corner, Hyde Park, today there was one particular meeting that went off quite comfortably. It was the National Old Age Pensioners' Association meeting, and the pensioners attending decided to take things very comfortably by relaxing in deck chairs to listen to the speakers'.

Round Pond maintenance, December 1969

Caption on reverse – 'Round Pond being cleaned. The Round Pond, Kensington Gardens, an imaginary sea for generations of model boat-sailing enthusiasts, looked more like a dry dock yesterday for James and Sandy Swinton of nearby Palace Gate'.

Lakes and ponds require constant de-silting, re-lining and debris removal, entailing unavoidable inconvenience. Recent finds include unexploded bombs, cars and supermarket trolleys.

247

Speakers' Corner, Hyde Park, 1971

We are fortunate to have inherited these wonderful heritage parks that give so much pleasure to so many. Sadly, this popularity, and insufficient recognition of the consequent pressures, may leave future generations poorer. It is hoped that the gentleman is mistaken.

LIST OF EXHIBITS AND ILLUSTRATIONS

LIST OF EXHIBITS AND ILLUSTRATIONS

1 PARK FORMATION AND DEVELOPMENT

1   Richard Blome (1635-1705), *A Mapp of ye County of Middlesex with its Hundreds*, 1673. Hand-coloured copper engraving, 28 x 37.5. © The Hearsum Collection 2017.

2   John Speed (1552-1629), *Surrey Described and Divided into Hundreds*, 1610. Hand-coloured copper engraving, 53.2 x 66.3. © The Hearsum Collection 2017.

3   Robert Girdler, *The Parish of Kilmainham in the County of Dublin*, Down Survey Map, 1650 (NLI 714 P7382). Photographic reproduction, 50.8 x 121.5. Courtesy of the National Library of Ireland.

4   John Michael Wright (1617-94) (in the style of), *James Butler (1610-88), 1st Duke of Ormonde, KG.* Oil on canvas, 123 x 101. State Art Collection, OPW.

5   Thomas Taylor, *A Survey of the part of Newtowne and Kilmainham left out of the Phoenix Park ..., Dublin, 1671*, 32.3 x 27.5 (NLI MS 16.G.17 [48]). Courtesy of the National Library of Ireland.

6   William III (1650-1702), *On the deer in Hide Park.* From the Court at Kensington, 1 June 1699. The manuscript document is addressed to Edward, Earl of Jersey. Manuscript, 30.5 x 20. © The Hearsum Collection 2017.

7   Stephen Slaughter (1697-1765), *Philip Dormer Stanhope, 4th Earl of Chesterfield, Lord Lieutenant of Ireland 1745-46.* Oil on canvas, 125.5 x 100, State Art Collection, OPW.

8   Leonard Knyff (1650-1722), engraved by Johannes Kip (1653-1722), *New Park, 1709 (Richmond Park).* Hand-coloured copper engraving, 17.5 x 24. From John Bowles, *Prospects of All the Cathedral and Collegiate Churches of England and Wales.*

9   *Breaching the wall in Richmond Park on 16 May 1751. Woodcut*, 10.8 x 16, from *Two Historical Accounts ... of New Forest and Richmond New Park.*

10 Thomas Stewart (date unknown), engraved by R. Field, *John Lewis of Richmond*, 1793. Aquatint, 37 x 27.

11 James Asser, *A Drawing of His Majesty's Park The Phenix in the Kingdom of Ireland, Dublin, c. 1775,* , 36.6 x 47. Courtesy of the American Embassy.

12 John Henry Campbell (1757-1828) (attributed to), *The Under-secretary's lodge, Phoenix Park, Dublin, 1755-1828.* Oil on canvas, 45 x 60. Courtesy of the late C.E.W. Trench, Slane, Co.Meath.

13 *Pembroke Lodge, Richmond Park*, 1847, News magazine woodcut, 29.5 x 17.4, *Illustrated London News.*

14 *The Viceregal Lodge...Deer Grazing on Front Lawn, Phoenix Park, Dublin*, unsigned and undated but pre-1835. Print, 23 x 30 (NGI, PD 942 TB). Collection National Gallery of Ireland. Photo © National Gallery of Ireland.

15 *The Chestnuts and the Diana Fountain, Bushy Park*, 1876. Woodcut, 31.7 x 24.2, from *Picturesque Europe, The Forest Scenery of Great Britain* (Cassell, London,1876).

16 Unknown artist, 18th century (after John Maurer (act.1713-1761)), published by Laurie and Whittle, *St James's Park, taken near the stable yard, 1794.* Hand-coloured copper engraving, 26 x 39.

17 *The Queen's Palace, Pimlico, Middlesex (with Marble Arch), c.1842.* Hand- coloured steel engraving, 8 x 11, from Thomas Dugdale, *Curiosities of Great Britain: England and Wales Delineated* (Tallis, London).

18 Sir Edwin Henry Landseer, RA (1802-1873) (attributed to), *A View in Richmond Park (Study)*, 1844. Oil on canvas, 21 x 31. © The Hearsum Collection 2017.

19 Decimus Burton (1800-1881), *Ashtown Gate, Phoenix Park... No 2. design for the proposed lodge..., Dublin, 1839*, 65.3 x 47.5 (NLI 2121). Courtesy of the National Library of Ireland.

20 *The Zoological Gardens, Regent's Park, c.1851.* Hand coloured steel engraving, 10.5 x 15. From *Tallis's Illustrated London*, 1851.

21 Sworn statement by witness Captain Richard Cobham, signed by Justice of the Peace Rodney Fane, of a fatal sword duel in Hyde Park in December 1700, when Captain Robert Swift killed Colonel Edward Dutton Colt. Manuscript, 20 x 16. © The Hearsum Collection 2017.

LIST OF EXHIBITS AND ILLUSTRATIONS

46 HM Queen Elizabeth II planting an oak tree at the Peace Bell in the grounds of Áras an Uachtaráin, in the presence of the President of Ireland Mary McAleese on 17 May 2011. Maxwell Photography. Courtesy of President's Office, Áras an Uachtaráin.

3 MILITARY AND THE WAR YEARS

47 *Plan of manoeuvres performed in the Phoenix Park in June 1775, ordered by General Irwine*, photographic reproduction, 88 x 73.4, Royal Collection Trust/© Her Majesty Queen Elizabeth II 2017 (RCIN 734007).

48 Gabriel Beranger (1725-1817) (probable designer), 'Volunteer Fabric' representing the provincial review of the Irish Volunteers of the province of Leinster which took place in the Phoenix Park in June 1782. Linen and cotton, 124.5 x 74.9. Courtesy of the Castletown Foundation.

49 Thomas Malton (1748-1804), after Thomas Rowlandson (1756-1827), *A Field Day in Hyde Park, 1789*. Coloured aquatint, 24 x 35. Published by SW Fores, London, 15 May 1789.

50 Giovanni Antonio Canal (called Canaletto) (1697-1768), engraved by Thomas Bowles, *A View of the Parade in St James's Park, The New Buildings for the Horse Guards, The Admiralty with His Majesty going to the House of Lords, 1753*. Published Laurie and Whittle, 12 May 1794. Hand-coloured copper engraving, 26 x 39.

51 Lieut. P. Cary, *A View of the Royal Military Infirmary, Phoenix Park, from the Royal Hospital, Dublin*, probably 1792. Collection of the Royal Hospital, Chelsea; photographic reproduction by kind permission.

52 Richard Earlom (1743-1822), after a drawing by Robert Smirke (1780-1867), *King George III Reviewing the Volunteer Corps assembled in Hyde Park in honour of his Birthday, 1799*. Coloured aquatint, 62 x 88.

53 *A Field Day in the Phoenix Park, 8 May 1843*. Print published by W Kohler, 22 Denmark Street, Dublin. Photograph by Motoko Fujita, 30 x 44. Private collection.

54 *The Meteorological Observatory in Phoenix Park, 1856*, plate from John Cameron, *Meteorological Observations taken during the years 1829 to 1852, at the Ordnance Survey Office*, London, 35.1 x 25.3.

55 Guards Army manoeuvres in Hyde Park, 1915. Photograph, 16.5 x 21.5, Keystone Press Agency Ltd.

56 Hyde Park Corner searchlight, 1914, *The Illustrated War News*, 40 x 29.

57 Winston Churchill in a sailor suit, dated 1878, and with his aunt Lady Leslie in Dublin 1880. Reproduced with permission of Curtis Brown Ltd., London, on behalf of the Broadwater Collection.

58 J H Oughton (1913-1969), *Planned air raid shelter for a million people beneath Hyde Park, 1938*. Photograph, 18 x 23, Wide World Photo.

59 A barrage balloon, Hyde Park, 1943. Photograph, 18 x 23, ACME Photo.

60 A baby with his personal gas mask, Hyde Park, 1939. Photograph, 18 x 23, ACME Photo.

61 The air raid trenches in Green Park, 1940. Photograph, 18 x 23, ACME Photo.

62 Fire Brigade practice, Hyde Park, 1941. Photograph, 27 x 17.5, International News Photos.

63 Hyde Park as a salvage depot, wood salvaged from the Blitz, 1941. Photograph, 18 x 23, ACME Photo.

64 The Phantom Squad in Richmond Park. GHQ Liaison Regiment (known as Phantom) a reconnaissance unit, 1941. Photograph, 28 x 21, Source: Colonel DTW Gibson.

65 A model for Peter Pan returns. Lance-Corporal J W Shaw, who operates the searchlight in an anti-aircraft division, with Peter Pan statue, Kensington Gardens, 1941. Photograph, 23 x 18, ACME Photo.

66 Now that the railings are gone. Lunch Hour – enjoying the grass as railings have been removed to make munitions, St James's Park, 1942. Photograph, 18 x 23, Associated Press.

67 An unusual sight: American soldiers demonstrating in the Serpentine, 1943. Photograph, 18 x 23, ACME Photo.

68 The aftermath of war: the bomb that ticked in St James's Park, 1946, *Illustrated London News*, 29 x 40.

LIST OF EXHIBITS AND ILLUSTRATIONS

95 AC Cooper and Victor Horsley
    BS, FRS, 'An outbreak of rabies
    in Richmond Park, 1888'. Report
    presented to both Houses of
    Parliament by command of Her
    Majesty. Published by Eyre and
    Spottiswoode.

96 Books of Regulations, Bye Laws and
    Deer Accounts, OPW.

97 The Dogs' Acre (Dog Cemetery)
    Hyde Park, 1899, *The Sketch*, 35 x
    25.

98 Headstone for Jack, King
    Edward VII's dog. Modern digital
    photograph by Motoko Fujita.
    Courtesy of the President's Office,
    Áras an Uachtaráin.

99 Police control Oswald Mosley's
    Fascist rally, Hyde Park, 1934.
    Photograph, 18 x 22.5, ACME
    Photos.

100 Parkgate Street Police Barracks
    handover and Park Constable / Park
    Ranger cap Badges. Photograph
    courtesy of the Manning Family; cap
    badges courtesy of OPW Collection.

101 Gas light and lamplighter in the
    Phoenix Park c. 1974. Photograph by
    Ian Finlay.

102 The Achilles statue is cleaned, Hyde
    Park, 1934. Photograph, 23 x 18,
    Associated Press NY.

103 Sheep in Kensington Gardens, 1949.
    Photograph, 20 x 25.5.

104 Feeding the deer in Richmond Park,
    1956. Photograph, 21 x 26, Keystone
    Press NYC.

105 Rag Week students battle with
    police, Hyde Park, 1966. Photograph,
    20 x 25.5, Keystone Press NYC.

106 Tree planting in Richmond Park,
    1970s. Photograph, 22 x 24, Roy
    Cook Photography.

107 A demonstration with a difference,
    Hyde Park, 1969. Photograph, 20 x
    25, Keystone Press Agency.

108 The Round Pond being cleaned
    (emptied for the first time in 43
    years), Kensington Gardens, 1969.
    Photograph, 20.5 x 25, Keystone
    Press Agency.

109 Famous Last Words? Speakers'
    Corner, Hyde Park, 1971. Photograph,
    29 x 20.5, AP Newsfeatures.

'I am unwilling to leave the world
a worse place than I found it.'
Timothy Bennett, 1754

PARKS

Our Shared Heritage

The Phoenix Park, Dublin
& The Royal Parks, London

OPW
Oifig na nOibreacha Poiblí
The Office of Public Works

THE HEARSUM
COLLECTION

THE
ROYAL
PARKS

PARKS

Our Shared Heritage